MANAGE YOUR
OWN CAREER

MANAGE YOUR OWN CAREER
A Self-Help Guide to Career Choice and Change

Ben Ball

Published by The British Psychological Society
and Kogan Page Ltd

First published in 1989 by The British Psychological Society, St Andrews House, 48 Princess Road East, Leicester, LE1 7DR in association with Kogan Page, London.

Reprinted 1992

British Library Cataloguing in Publication Data

```
Ball, Ben
  Manage your own career: a self-help guide to
  Career choice and change.
  1. Great Britain, Careers. Planning - Mannuals
  I. Title
  331.7'02'0941
```

ISBN 1 85091 861 9

Set in Linotype Palatino
by Arrow Photoset, Leicester
Printed and bound in Great Britain by BPCC Wheatons Ltd, Exeter.

Whilst every effort has been made to ensure the accuracy of the contents of this publication, the publishers and authors expressly disclaim responsibility in law for negligence or any other cause of action whatsoever.

CONTENTS

CONTENTS

INTRODUCTION

This book is about career choice and change. It is for people of all ages: people thinking about a change in mid career, people just about to leave education, in fact, anyone thinking about their future career.

The message implicit in this book is that **you** can make career decisions and choices for **yourself**, based on your self knowledge, but with some constructive feedback from other people around you – family, friends and other people in and out of the workplace.

The method outlined is **career planning**. This is not, as it might seem, a way of planning away the next 35 years of your life, but quite simply a way of preparing for your next job move or career change by using a systematic approach. It is a process that allows you to be in control of life events by inviting you to take positive action on your own behalf to start/change/improve your working life. The process of career planning may also help to improve your motivation, confidence or sense of self worth. Implicit in this process are three kinds of activity:

1. **career planning** is about reviewing your past experience of education, work and life events to identify what you have learned and achieved to date and the people and events that have influenced your life.

2. **career planning** is to do with pinpointing your present situation, your interests, skills and values, and making clear what you would like to change.

3. **career planning** is concerned with implementing ideas, setting goals for the future, and achieving the kind of changes you would like to see happening in your life.

The book contains examples and case studies designed to help you through the planning process. Further reading is also suggested. *Bonne chance!*

Stages in Career Planning

Start here ▶

REVIEW

Market yourself

Go for interviews

Make applications

Identify employers or courses

Look in depth at options

Implement ideas — Take action

Decide on possible options

Gather ideas

PROMOTER

RESEARCHER

EXPLORER

DESIGNER

START

Review past experiences

Analyse skills

Assess your values

Design your personal profile

Invite feedback

Check job interests

PART 1

ALL CHANGE AT THE WORKPLACE

▼ What's been happening in the job market?

▼ Where will the new jobs be?

▼ Implications for job seekers

▼ Changing our notions of 'career'

▼ Making initial career choices

▼ Self employment and the small business

▼ Making mid career changes

▼ There is more to work than a job

▼ Where are you in your thinking?

In the early 1980s when the world was plunged into economic recession and unemployment rates around the world were at their highest since the 1930s, a number of writers predicted the end of the age of full employment. We had, it seemed, passed into a post-industrial age in which the idea of paid employment for all was no longer tenable. The future of work, and in particular the full-time job, was under question. There needed to be radical responses to cope with a world without work.

Writers agreed that the work ethic needed to be replaced either by a leisure scenario – ways of sharing available work so that we could all enjoy more leisure – or a contribution ethic which would involve a redirection of people's energies to contribute to society's well-being rather than pursue economic growth in the traditional way. In the post-industrial society we needed to develop the idea of work with a more human dimension, work that was local and community based, less technologically oriented.

Since then, unemployment rates have stabilized. In many countries there has been a reduction in the number of those out of work and an upturn in levels of economic growth. Despite the challenge to our values provoked by the recession, work is still in most people's minds equated with the idea of a full-time job.

The age of leisure has patently not arrived. Time spent at work has not reduced significantly. There is no evidence of a major redistribution of working hours. Job sharing schemes have met with only limited success. On the basis of current trends, the average working week in the UK will still be roughly 37 hours by the end of the century.

If the total number of hours we spend at work has been reduced, this is largely because people are delaying entry into the labour market because of education and training, and also because of earlier retirement. On the basis of current trends then, leisure will not be a central feature of most people's lives – at least until the year 2000. For the majority, work, synonymous with paid employment, will be.

What's been happening in the job market?

For anyone reviewing the history of the 1980s, one major theme will recur: the impact of **economic recession** and of **technological change** on jobs and employment. For the early part of the decade the news from the job market was largely negative: increased

4

rates of redundancy and business failure led to an overall **job shortage** and **mass unemployment.** For many people the idea of permanent work or stable career became illusory. For others the search for work rested on the ability to make major life changes: in job, in location, in employment status.

Unemployment

Estimates vary about the true extent of unemployment. One fact, however, is clear: that for most of the last decade there was widespread unemployment, with the jobless total rising to three million or more in the UK, where unemployment rates were higher than in the United States, Japan and most countries in the European community.

Unemployment, of course, does not have a uniform impact. Some geographical areas have a far higher incidence than others, with the north of England and Northern Ireland being particularly hard hit, along with many inner city areas. Some groups are affected more than others and it is the unskilled and semiskilled who are most likely to suffer – over 60 per cent of unemployed males would fall into this category.

Two age groups have suffered most from the period of economic recession and job restructuring:

1. Young people aged between 16 and 19 have seen the virtual collapse of the youth job market and, as a group, have largely been withdrawn from the labour market as a result of government programmes of vocational preparation and training. What was once a typical feature of many young people's lives, the apprenticeship with a wage, has now been replaced with training programmes and training allowances with no guarantee of employment at the end. Between 1983 and 1987 nearly 20 per cent of all 18 year olds were out of a job at any one time.

2. Those aged 55 or more have also been prey to redundancy and early retirement packages. And although compulsory retirement ages are still 65 and 60 for men and women respectively, in practice the number of people actually staying in full-time employment until those ages gets smaller each year. Government programmes have encouraged this process still further.

However, things seem set to change. By 1994 there will be one million fewer 16–19 year olds than in 1987. Employment prospects will improve, for demographic reasons if for no other.

Job losses in manufacturing and the impact of technology

The manufacturing industries bore the brunt of the recession. Between 1981 and 1986 nearly 200,000 jobs were lost annually. Many of these job losses were in heavy industries such as shipbuilding and steel but other industries suffered also. One leading clothes manufacturer reduced its workforce from 20,000 to 3000 in seven years.

Further job losses in the manufacturing sector are predicted beyond 1990 as developments in new technology create the conditions for increased output from a smaller human workforce. Anyone who has seen an assembly line of robots in a car manufacturing plant, or seen how computer aided design has revolutionized the cutting room of a clothes manufacturer will also be aware of the power of technology to displace human workers. Automation can destroy jobs.

Exactly how many jobs have been lost by the uptake of modern technology is open to question. But the advance continues. In both manufacturing and processing industries, microelectronics reduce the need for manual workers and those concerned with maintenance and repair.

The skill shortage

Many people find it difficult to believe that at a time of mass unemployment there can be jobs on offer and no one to fill them. And yet this was the case throughout the recession of the 1980s. And these were not low-paid jobs which no one wanted to do, but highly-paid jobs requiring high level skills. There has, for example, been a nationally recognized shortage of people with skills related to computing, computer manufacture and electronics – what is often called information technology. Programmers, systems analysts, software engineers and electronic engineers of all kinds continue to be in desperately short supply. Many of these jobs are at a professional level. But there is also a shortage amongst those with related technical skills, in testing and servicing equipment. At a general level the message is clear – those with high levels of transferable skill are easily employed.

Obvious evidence for this is provided by the example of graduate employment. Between 1985 and 1988 it became clear that one group of people would have few problems in finding full-time jobs – new graduates. At the same time as the recorded unemployment total hovered around three million, 100,000 new graduates each year left universities and polytechnics, most of whom readily found employment. Graduates in accountancy, business studies, computing, engineering of all kinds, architecture, building and subjects related to medicine were all in high demand and continue to be so.

Where will the new jobs be?

There are two ways of looking at job futures. One is to assess the growth potential of various business sectors, for example, retailing. The other is to analyse the kinds of skill that are likely to be most in demand in the post-industrial society.

It is clear that on the basis of current trends, job growth will take place largely in the **service sector** of the economy – all those activities and businesses concerned with the provision of personal and industrial services. The following seven business sectors, for example, are all set to expand still further in terms of job growth: hotels and catering, banking, insurance, building societies, business services, wholesale distribution and retailing.

It is important to realize that the service sector is not simply about providing services to individual consumers – meals and hotel rooms, hairdressing and car valeting. It is also to do with providing companies and industrial clients with a whole range of specialized services that they will want to contract out rather than do in-house – staff recruitment, advertising, printing, catering, cleaning, landscape and building maintenance. These 'intermediate' services will also expand in terms of jobs. There will of course be many others. Given the age profile of the population, *health care*, whether public or private, is going to be a major provider of jobs; so too are *social services* generally. Many people will also be employed in *security services*, as well as in the *communications media*.

On the debit side there are likely to be continuing job losses in agriculture, engineering and manufacturing generally. From the career planning perspective, however, it is important to avoid making too many assumptions on the basis of such trends. It needs to be emphasized that manufacturing industry, for example, will continue to employ millions of people for the foreseeable future. Well over two million workers are still employed in the engineering industry alone. There will be job growth, particularly amongst smaller manufacturing companies as their businesses expand.

Most job growth, then, will take place in the service sector, but what kinds of occupation will this include? Which work activity will take on increasing importance? The table summarizes the range of jobs which will be in high demand and where, in some cases, there will be pronounced shortages of qualified personnel.

THE CHANGING JOB MARKET

◀ ◀ ◀ Expanding occupations ▶ ▶ ▶

All professions: accountants, architects, doctors, surveyors, engineers and scientists of all descriptions.

Technologists and technicians working in the production industries, particularly those related to information technology.

Health care occupations: physiotherapists, radiologists, etc.

▶ ▶ ▶ Contracting occupations ◀ ◀ ◀

Single skill craftspeople in industry

Factory operatives

Farm labourers

Unskilled and semiskilled manual workers

Full-time jobs in personal services

In general there will be an increased need for **'knowledge' workers** (workers who are paid to think rather than perform routine tasks) in all sectors of the economy. Biotechnologists, quantity surveyors, building services engineers, business consultants, market research analysts each have a different knowledge base but will all be in demand because of the *level* of skill and professional expertise they provide. Other factors, however, may play a part. Opportunities for teachers may decline in total because of the falling birth rate. But this could well be offset by the increased demand for professional *'trainers'* to work either in or outside the education system to provide opportunities for adult education and training.

One major area of job growth will be associated with the

computerization of all aspects of working life. **Information technology** is an umbrella term used to describe electronics, computing and data processing. It is likely to be one of the biggest areas of job growth until well into the next decade, but is a highly technical area requiring skilled personnel. The range of employing organizations is vast. At one end of the spectrum there are the microchip and computer manufacturers; at the other end is the small computer user. In between are the electronics companies who employ thousands of staff in the design and development of products with microchip components, the array of companies who use computers for business and office systems such as payroll, stores inventory and accounting, and the computer consultancies which design and install new systems and software.

Within electronics companies there will be an increasing demand for software engineers, communications engineers and electronics engineers, as well as sales and marketing specialists. In the computer departments of user companies there will be recruitment of programmers and systems analysts.

Two other types of job emerge from the computerization of the office. First, there is an increasing need for business system *consultants* to advise companies on what kind of computer system to buy and install, for example, for accounting purposes, or for hotel reservations. Second, there is a need for *trainers* – people to train others in the use of computers in the home or at the workplace. This activity is often called 'end user support' and relies heavily on people who have good interpersonal skills. Information technology is therefore a major source of new jobs.

Implications for job seekers

Apart from the profound consequences of high rates of unemployment, what are the implications for job seekers of the trends that have taken place in the job market? One is that **change and uncertainty** is a major underlying force with which we all have to cope, as new jobs appear and old ones disappear, as some industries recede in importance and others emerge. We are forced to make adaptive responses. Few people can predict the exact nature of the job market in, say, ten years, but if we have learned anything from the experience of the 1980s, it is that **flexibility** and **adaptability** are vital watchwords for those who want to remain in employment or create their own successful working ventures.

Certainly companies and employers have become more flexible in the way they employ staff to reduce their overheads. Where they can, managers will *contract work out* to other firms and individuals rather than employ their own full-time staff. They will employ *part-time* rather than full-time staff, *temporary* workers as well as permanent. At the centre of many business organizations, for example, there will now be a core of permanent staff enjoying the full range of staff benefits, and working alongside them, a range of temporary, contract or part-time staff, enjoying fewer perks and a shorter employment horizon, with little or no company commitment to training, staff development and so on.

This trend has particular implications. If you are employed on a short-term contract, you may have fewer rights and employment benefits, are more likely to be laid off without prior consultation, have a sense of uncertainty about your future. On the positive side, there can be advantages. Being able to hire your labour for only part of the year, or at certain times of the year, gives you more discretionary time for leisure and other interests. The lesson, however, is clear. The more flexible the employers become in recruiting and employing staff, the more flexible individual workers need to be to adjust to the new practices.

The drive towards greater flexibility on the employers' part has given rise to one remarkable trend in the job market: the increase in part-time employment. At the end of the 1980s much of the growth of new jobs was in part-time work, benefiting women workers more than men, since many of the new jobs were created in the service sector. Significantly, between 1979 and 1987 the total number of full-time workers decreased by more than a million. The number of part-time workers increased by the same amount. This noticeable trend is obviously encouraged by employers and at the same time is a manifestation of changing social aspirations as women participate more in the labour market.

Finally, the most obvious consequence of the impact of technology on jobs, the development of 'high tech' products and the push for economic competitiveness is that our level of job related skills needs regularly updating. Any investment we as individuals can make in education and training is therefore going to be a good thing. The technological change that is taking place in all sectors of industry, the automation that is affecting the service sector of the economy, will change the nature and complexity of jobs on offer. On balance, more workers will require *higher skill levels* than before. There is a clear equation between high levels of skill and the prospect of employment.

Changing our notions of 'career'

Changes in the main economy influence our ideas about what is possible and how we can direct our lives. In particular, change and increased rates of technological change provide us with a new set of assumptions about careers, employment and work. The notion of career has certainly undergone some serious challenges.

'There is such a thing as a job for life'

The idea that individuals stay with 'the company' for the whole of their working lives without any changes has been seriously challenged by recent events. People will need in future to be prepared for a more interrupted career pattern, recognizing that a number of job and career changes may be necessary to give them the job satisfaction they need. For some, periods of employment will be interspersed with periods of unemployment. For others, work will be comprised of a number of different part-time jobs, various forms of contract work or periods of temporary work. For still others there will be the prospect of long-term unemployment, a jobless future.

'Career is a sequence of 'better' jobs'

For many people the word 'career' implies a series of jobs, each one involving more responsibility or better pay; a pattern of upward mobility. The 'tea boy to managing director' story was never the reality for the majority of the working population and is now even more remote. The hierarchical nature of most organizations ensures that a few people reach the top, whilst the majority perform other, less well paid work. By no means everyone will be able to progress up the promotion ladder. For many, career development will be a series of sideways moves – going to a different company, but doing the same job; moving to a different, but similar status job within the same company. For others, there will be apparently downward moves. The fifty-year-old redundant executive may have difficulty going to a job of similar status and be prepared to settle for something less demanding.

11

'Career relates only to jobs and employment'

For those on the fringes of full-time employment and on the periphery of large organizations, career development may be concerned with balancing a variety of roles and work demands. For those women, particularly, who interrupt employment for family reasons, 'career' will be concerned with childrearing, part-time paid work and possibly voluntary work. Career development will take in family, personal and community roles. The 'career break' will increasingly be a time for continued professional updating by distance learning. The re-entry to employment will be characterized by flexible hours and/or job share schemes.

'The organization can do it all for you'

Many large organizations in the past have attempted to 'manage' the careers of their staff. Personnel managers recruit and promote staff to new jobs, management development specialists decide on training and experience 'packages' to promote their 'high fliers' and junior managers on the 'fast track'. Ultimately, however, individuals need to take hold of their own work futures. They need to be on the look out for training and job opportunities that will provide self development.

IN SUMMARY . . .

Traditional assumption	Emerging assumption
Full employment is sustainable	▶ Full employment is not likely to return in the foreseeable future
Most people follow a stable, straight-line career path to retirement	▶ Career paths are increasingly going to be diverted and interrupted
Career development means upward mobility	▶ Career development can be facilitated by lateral and downward moves
Only new or young employees can be developed	▶ Learning and change can occur at any age and career stage
Career development relates primarily to work experience and can only take place in one's job	▶ Career development is influenced by family, personal and community roles, and can be facilitated by work outside paid employment

Making initial career choices

For those at 16 plus, career decisions are often linked to *educational* choices. Finding a full-time job or a place on a Youth Training Scheme for experience-based training raises immediate questions of career choice and commitment to a particular kind of work. By contrast, staying on at school or going to college to take A level, Certificate of Pre-Vocational Education, or repeat GCSE examinations leave students the possibility of postponing career decisions a little longer. A further option, that of taking a job related, full-time course at a college of further education may well call for some, at least tentative, career decisions.

At 18 plus, the options are similar. Students can look for work which may lead to part-time training or, with the right qualifications, go on to higher education at college, polytechnic or university.

In some cases there may be two routes leading to the same level of job. Becoming a surveyor, training for retail management or starting a career in financial services, can be embarked on at the A level stage or after studying for a degree. In other cases it will be essential to study for a first degree. Becoming a pharmacist, architect or professional engineer will usually require a full-time course of study to graduate level.

For all students leaving education, the question of what to do will be influenced by individual interests and ambitions, but choices will also be moderated by three factors: **field**, **level** and **labour market**.

The subjects of study you enjoy most and are best at may well influence the choice of job **field**. For example, company-based engineering training schemes will be open to those who have a strong profile in maths and science subjects. Those who show more aptitude for creative and design subjects may well look towards vocational training in the art and design field. Your main subject of study, your best subjects at school, may well initially determine the kind of work or further education you choose.

At the same time, the **level** of your existing qualifications will provide you with entry requirements for different levels of work and training. For example, anyone interested in accountancy work will need good GCSE passes to become an accounting technician, but A levels or a degree to become a professional accountant. In computing, those with good GCSE results can become computer operators. To work as a programmer, however, you will normally need a Business and Technical Education Council (BTEC) Higher Diploma in computer studies, or a degree.

Finally, the availability of jobs and training opportunities will obviously depend on what options are available in the local and national **labour market.** For those leaving school at 16 plus who do not opt for further full-time education, the availability of local jobs and or YTS placements may be a critical factor in determining the early stages of a person's career.

❛JANE *left school with O levels in English language and literature, maths and home economics, CSEs in geography and chemistry. Not wanting to stay on at school, she opted for a one-year secretarial/personal assistants' course at the local technical college, studying bookkeeping and some law at the same time. She then found a secretarial job with a local finance house and, after eight months was promoted to personnel assistant. She subsequently went to work for the BBC in London and later at the head office of a major retailing firm.* ❜

One of the main choice problems facing students leaving education is to do with a lack of work sampling experience. They will say 'How can I decide what to do next when I have no experience on which to base my decision? I have not tested myself against anything'. One way to overcome this is to do some of the career planning exercises which follow. For many students, however, it takes a spell of work experience to bring things in to sharper focus.

❛TERRY *graduated in biology and chemistry. He landed a job with a top advertising agency, selling advertising space in magazines, but after six months was extremely disenchanted. It was not for him.*

One evening he presented the problem to his flatmates, and they sat around to discuss Terry's future. What were his interests? There were a number, but one in particular: beer. He liked drinking it and was interested in how it was made. Six months later, he was a trainee brewer with a leading firm, and about to be sponsored on a postgraduate course in brewing science. ❜

The case studies illustrate the links between qualifications, type of job and the relevance of training. But what about people in mid career who want to move on to something better, but may not have relevant qualifications?

This is a serious problem for many adults. It is difficult to get hold of information about the careers and courses that are available, extremely difficult to get any financial support for full-time study, and there are major problems in finding out whether they might be exempt from formal entry qualifications for occupations and courses of training.

❛JILL *left school at 15 without taking any O levels. After 14 years of clerical and typing work, much of it temporary, she was desperate to find a way out, but without qualifications or the 'right' experience, found that she was trapped. She found herself 'going round in circles' trying to get information and advice. Eventually some friends told her about a course which encouraged applications from 'mature' students: the Diploma in Management Studies at the local polytechnic. Because of her lack of formal qualifications she had to take a special entrance exam as well as pass the interview. She succeeded in getting a place. At the age of 29, she was on course as a mature student.* ❜

Self employment and the small business

For many people, getting established in the workplace is not so much about choosing a job, but about putting their skills and interests to work by working for themselves. In the UK, three million people are self employed. The government is keen to help would-be entrepreneurs by special employment measures. As a result, more and more people are choosing to work for themselves. For some professional groups, e.g. accountants and architects, self employment has always been the norm, but they are being joined by a host of others, either because full-time jobs do not exist or because their entrepreneurial skills would otherwise be wasted. Artists, designers, builders, business consultants, contract caterers, landscape gardeners and wordsmiths of all kinds have one thing in common: they work for themselves.

There are problems, of course, for the novice: raising initial business finance, finding premises where necessary, keeping accounts and financial records, sorting out taxation problems, marketing your services, and the day-to-day problems of time management. And, of course, there is always the risk of being without work, of business failure. For many people self employment is simply a precursor to running your own business – growing in size and employing other people.

❛STUART'S *career started with a variety of jobs: fireplace fitter, articled clerk, kitchen fitter and tour leader for an adventure holiday company. After studying for a history degree, he worked for five years as a self employed kitchen fitter, trading on the skills he had developed earlier and reinforced by the family business: selling kitchens. Kitchen fitting was a good antidote to university which provided a reasonable income and enjoyable end results. On the negative side there were taxation problems and no holidays for three years. From fitting, he moved on to designing and planning kitchens and other products. With a colleague he successfully designed and produced a bicycle trailer, which went into regular production. After that, the move to retail premises provided the opportunity to launch a company supplying and fitting ready-made kitchen and bedroom furniture. Turnover has doubled annually and the business now has two full-time employees.*

Making mid career changes

As we saw earlier, mid career changes are becoming increasingly common as people respond to the caprices of the job market or else search for further personal development.

Two responses to redundancy

The impact of redundancy can be devastating and can bring about a host of negative consequences for the individual concerned. Sometimes, however, redundancy can provide individuals with a welcome opportunity to review their lives and take off in a new direction. Some use redundancy pay to become self employed or to start their own business. For others it provides the excuse to make a career change that they had been putting off for some time.

KEN had been employed as a laboratory technician and was made redundant by British Steel in 1979. Thereafter followed two difficult years of dole, short-term work and all the negative feelings associated with unemployment. It was then that he decided to study for two A levels at the local technical college. Accountancy was his best subject and he passed with sufficiently high grades to study on a BA accountancy course at a polytechnic.

In some instances, early retirement is a way of making individuals redundant. But taking voluntary redundancy in your early 50s is one way of avoiding some of the bitterness, frustration and financial loss which characterizes forced redundancies.

ALAN had been a teacher of physical education and later lectured at a teacher education centre. With the reduction of places for trainee teachers in the early 1980s, he opted for early retirement. He thus had the opportunity to do something he had wanted to do all his life – to 'do the knowledge' and become a taxi driver. He now owns his own cab and has a thriving business which supplements his retirement income.

Career change at 40

Career changes, of course, are not restricted to people in their early 20s or those taking early retirement. Occasionally, the 'mid life crisis' can bring about a major review of life and career, leading to some dramatic changes of direction for the individuals concerned.

❛DON HENDERSON had a string of different jobs: dental technician, police officer, ice-cream seller, pharmaceutical sales rep. He had always been involved in amateur theatre and one day, for a dare, he went for an audition at the Royal Shakespeare Company in Stratford. At the age of 39 he was offered his first acting job and stayed with the RSC for six years. He then went on to create the character of retired police inspector Bulman in a long-running TV series.❜

© Dickinson. Reprinted by kind permission of the *Times Educational Supplement*.

Returning to work after a break

For many women who give up work to have children the key issue is 'What will I do when I return to work, and will the work be at the same level as I am used to?'. Having a career break brings with it many of the symptoms associated with unemployment, and perhaps the most commonly experienced is that of lack of confidence. Even a short break from the workplace can undermine feelings of self worth.

Frequently, however, the return to work is not to a permanent full-time job. Many women take on part-time work as their children gradually work their way through playgroup, nursery school and full-time education. In many instances, therefore, returning to work is a gradual process – a steady progression from part-time to full-time work.

We saw earlier that one remarkable trend in the job market is the way that opportunities for female part-time work have replaced traditional full-time male jobs. Part-time and freelance work provide an important vehicle for those having career breaks.

❛SHEILA worked in market research for a division of a large international company after graduation. During her career break to have children she maintained her contacts and continued to do freelance data reduction and report writing. Nine years (and three children) later, she wrote speculatively to a financial services company who subsequently employed her full-time to start up its own market research department.

The maintenance of her skills during the career break had ensured a relatively easy transition to full-time working, when her children were old enough.❜

There is more to work than a job

'Moonlighting' is often used as a pejorative term to describe work that is done in addition to paid employment, often in the 'black' or 'informal' economy. In some communities there is a great deal of informal economic activity, even when there is plenty of paid employment. In some countries (Italy is normally cited as a classic example), the black economy can be an important aspect of economic life.

For many people, the economic reality is that wages from paid employment are not enough to sustain them and their families. They are forced to take on additional part-time work to supplement their meagre earnings from full-time employment. Other people have other reasons for taking on additional work. They may find their present job taps just a small part of their energy and ability and they therefore look for other ways of making life interesting. They get work satisfaction from their job *and* other work activities.

‘MARTIN *left the army and went into agriculture. After a number of years of looking after livestock, of getting up early to do the milking, of being 'on call' for most of the daylight hours, he decided to find a more structured life with a regular working week. He became a farming instructor at a residential centre for the mentally handicapped. The reduced number of hours in employment gave him the opportunity to engage in work that was previously a hobby, and he now has his own business setting up discos and public address systems, in addition to his full-time job.* ’

Where are you in your thinking?

The case studies illustrate one particular message: that career changes are now a normal feature of most people's lives, so that we all have to adapt to new circumstances, by finding opportunities to satisfy our career and work needs.

Of course, making changes in working life is not always a matter of starting a completely new career. It may be that a small change is what we need. Doing a similar job with a different employer or doing a different job with the same employer may give us the variety and new stimulus we require. We can make low risk, slight adjustments to our working lives. Alternatively, we might decide to develop ourselves rather than the job we do by expanding other leisure or life interests, by developing our personal rather than our job related skills.

What follows is largely for job seekers, those thinking about careers for the first time or those who are restarting or reconsidering their career. Working through the **Designer, Explorer, Researcher** and **Promoter** stages of the career planning process will be helpful in making specific your career goals or in reinforcing ideas you may already have entertained.

The more firmly you state your career plans, the more likely it is that you will be successful in putting them into practice.

Where are you in your thinking?

PART 2

CAREER CHOICE AND PLANNING

▼ Waiting for the 'lucky' break

▼ Is there one ideal job for each of us?

▼ Are there experts who can tell us what that ideal job is?

▼ Is it possible to change career direction?

▼ Designing a Personal and Career Profile

Waiting for the 'lucky' break

When you ask people to account for their career success, they may explain it in terms of their circumstances, or they may attribute their success to 'just a lucky break'. Did they have no real part to play in their success? Their hard work, their previous training and experience, their ability to take risks, their use of personal contacts in identifying openings and opportunities are minimized in this account of life events. Luck may have some part to play in the proceedings, but most individuals have the power to create opportunities for themselves by using appropriate skills (and that is the part that is often underplayed).

People have a number of other misconceptions about jobs and careers.

Is there one ideal job for each of us?

On the contrary, we are multi-potential. There are lots of jobs we could do given the opportunity or the access to training. As our work experience accumulates we tend to specialize in a given field and see ourselves in one particular role. But we each possess a range of skills that can be used in many different workplaces and there is a wide variety of jobs we could do. Career planning is to do with identifying which of these possibilities is appropriate for a given moment in time.

Are there experts who can tell us what that ideal job is?

The main task of careers advisers is to help **you** decide on a suitable career. They may present you with some possible options, but the final choice is yours. Some specialized careers guidance agencies use a range of psychological tests and may be able to pinpoint job areas into which you might fit, but they are unable to highlight the *one* job which can bring you ultimate success. In the main, therefore, the task of careers advisers and careers counsellors is to help **you** to come to a decision of **your own** making about which course to take, what job to do, and so on. The final choice is **yours**.

22

Is it possible to change career direction?

As you have seen in the previous section, it is perfectly possible to change your career path. You may encounter some major difficulties in doing so, but it is possible. As our experience increases, our needs change and this prompts us to review our situation. Some careers writers have predicted that many of us will undertake two or possibly three major occupational career changes – not simply job changes within the same occupation – during our lives. When we do so, it is important to remember that prior work experience and skills previously acquired will never be wasted. They have a cumulative effect, and when people change career direction, they often build on their previous knowledge, skills and experience.

So how do you go about the business of career choice and planning?

It is helpful to see **career planning** in terms of four interrelated stages.

1. *Stage 1* is the **Designer Stage**.

You begin by assessing your career needs. You define your **skills**, your **work values** and your **interests** and sort out some basic facts about **you**, that will help you define the kind of work you would like to do. At a basic level, jobs can be divided into three kinds:

those concerning *data*

those involving *people*

those involving *things*.

Many jobs will, of course, have an element of all three, but you may already have a hunch about which means most to you.

At the end of Stage 1, you will have designed a **Personal and Career Profile** – a list of your qualities, your needs and the kind of things you would like to find in your work.

2. *Stage 2* is the **Explorer Stage.**

You spend time exploring possible options: are you looking for a course of study/training or an immediate job? Which career options are possible? Which companies and organizations are recruiting?

Friends, family, careers advisers, tutors can all be useful in providing you with job ideas and suggestions. In fact, the grapevine is crucial for giving you useful information and ideas. Some careers agencies have computer programmes to help you in providing job ideas. At the end of this stage you should have a list of possible ideas – **a prospects list** – on which you can work further.

3. *Stage 3* is the **Researcher Stage.**

You take further the ideas from your **prospects list.** Spend time researching the ideas at length. Read company brochures, look at press articles, education and recruitment directories; get information from professional bodies. Find out where actual job vacancies are advertised.

Occasionally the amount of printed information is limited. It could be that there is no printed careers information on a particular option and you will have to seek advice directly from the companies concerned and from the professionals involved.

Some ideas will require considerable investigative research, and at the end you may start rejecting some of the ideas in your list. No matter. Others will come to the fore to take their place.

4. *Stage 4* is the **Promoter Stage.**

This is about **self marketing.** You start making applications, meeting potential employers, approaching training agencies or course centres.

Brushing up your communication skills will be important when composing a curriculum vitae or going for interview. As well as presenting yourself well in the selection process you will also need other communication skills, for example, in contacting personnel departments who may not have acknowledged your application or, possibly, in negotiating a starting salary.

24

If your self marketing is unsuccessful and you are not landing the interviews you want or getting any job offers, then it is time to seek expert help. Using the list of *Placement and Helping Agencies* on page 97-98 may be important now: it is a waste of your time to make lots of applications, only to get the same number of rejection letters.

Stage 1: Designing a Personal and Career Profile

You are asked to complete ten simple questionnaires about yourself – your skills, interests and values and the work you might be interested in doing – in a particular sequence. To begin with the focus is on you to give a personal profile and to re-assess where you are going in your career. After that the focus turns progressively towards the jobs you would like to do. The process invites you to review your ideas and then put them into clearer focus.

It will take about one hour to complete all the questionnaires properly, giving some thought to all the questions raised. You may find it helpful to go through the questionnaires with a friend or relative. This will take longer but the process will generate further ideas and discussion. Try and be as honest and as thorough as possible.

At the end of this section, you will not see the ideal job for you highlighted in the text, but you will have a specification, a blueprint for the kind of career that will meet your needs at this particular stage of your life. You will have a **Personal and Career Profile.** This can be matched with the job titles in any careers reference book (see *Information Sources*, pp.95ff.). The profile, of course, will change with time. Your circumstances will change. Your values may change. What seemed an interesting and demanding job one day, may, some months later, appear boring and routine. You will need to repeat the career planning process from time to time either to help you find fresh stimulus in your present job or to change to something else.

My achievements

In an employment orientated society, achievement is usually seen as related to work of some kind. And yet for many people their greatest achievements lie outside the workplace, for example running a half-marathon, bringing up a family, working for a charity or being an active member of a local community. People have diverse interests which provide scope for personal development and satisfaction.

Identify six things which have given you a real sense of achievement and pride, and about which you felt good. Use your whole experience from which to choose – events in your relationships with other people, educational achievements, activities at home or at work, and so on.

When you have identified your six achievements try and describe what each says about you as a person. For example, passing a driving test at the tenth attempt could say a lot about your perseverance!

As well as asking you to reflect on your past experience, the achievements exercise also has a more pragmatic purpose. When you start applying for jobs, you will be able to refer to it when filling in application forms and composing a curriculum vitae.

My interests

We all have interests: hobbies, sporting and social activities, topics we enjoy reading about, causes we campaign for. They are usually activities we engage in for their own sake, preferred ways of spending our time given the opportunity, things that we find intrinsically rewarding. Often, our interests will have something to say about us as people – the things we value most, our personalities, the kind of experiences and life events we have encountered – the life stage we have reached.

In Questionnaire Two, write down twelve of your main life interests – things you enjoy doing or care about. Review your list in five stages.

Questionnaire One

SIX THINGS OF WHICH I AM PROUD

My achievements   **What they say about me**

1. _____ ➡ _____

2. _____ ➡ _____

3. _____ ➡ _____

4. _____ ➡ _____

5. _____ ➡ _____

6. _____ ➡ _____

1. Try to assess **how long** you have been interested in the things you have itemized. Are they comparatively new activities or have you cultivated them over a number of years?

2. Next, consider the **amount of time** you devote to them. Are there any you would develop further if you had more time?

3. What **needs** do they satisfy? For example, someone who was interested in rock climbing or canoeing might say that their interest satisfied their need for strenuous physical activity along with an element of risk. By contrast, a member of a choral society might say that creative needs were being met along with the need for affiliation and contact with people.

4. Have your interests any **job significance?** For most people, interests are associated with leisure time, but some individuals also like to carry them over into paid employment or work of some kind. A persistent and time-consuming interest in *haute cuisine* might well lead someone to think of opening a restaurant. A lifelong interest in things horticultural might suggest the possibility of opening a garden centre.

5. Finally, highlight the three interests which are **most important** to you – those that are central to your life at present.

In reading through your list you may make some surprising discoveries – how little your interests have changed over time or how important some have become in your life. A particular pattern or line of development could be apparent which could have some significance to your overall career plan.

My skills

We often use the word 'skill' to describe competence at a fairly routine task. Driving a car is an obvious example. But for career planning we need to enlarge the definition of skill. Computer programming, graphic design and catering are all obvious examples of job related skills. It is also important to include those which may not at first sight have any particular vocational relevance. 'Being a good listener' is an important interpersonal skill. For those employed as nurses, doctors or personnel recruitment specialists it may not be an essential job requirement, but it could greatly add to the ability to do the job.

Questionnaire Two

MY MAIN INTERESTS

1. _____

2. _____

3. _____

4. _____

5. _____

6. _____

7. _____

8. _____

9. _____

10. _____

11. _____

12. _____

Questionnaire Three

MY SKILLS

	Score (6 = highest, 1 = lowest)

Creative

drawing, painting, design	☐
sensitivity to aesthetic values	☐
musical performance	☐
imagination	☐
creative writing	☐

Influencing

persuading/negotiating	☐
selling a product/service	☐
managing other people	☐
organizing events/activities	☐
promoting ideas effectively	☐

Communicating

using the written word	☐
translating foreign languages	☐
reporting on events	☐
speaking in public	☐
understanding written material	☐

Problem Solving

analysing information	☐
using maps and diagrams	☐
servicing equipment	☐
following detailed instructions	☐
assembling parts/components	☐

Physical

	Score
using hand/power tools	☐
operating plant/machinery	☐
manual dexterity	☐
physical stamina	☐
tending plants/animals	☐

Social

relating to a wide range of people	☐
giving help/support to others	☐
showing insight/understanding	☐
teaching/training	☐
building relationships	☐

Numerical

interpreting graphs/statistical reports	☐
handling/manipulating data	☐
using computers	☐
solving quantitative problems	☐
producing accounts/budgets	☐

SKILL AREA SCORE	TOTAL
Creative	☐
Influencing	☐
Communicating	☐
Problem Solving	☐
Physical	☐
Social	☐
Numerical	☐

Read through the Skills list (pp.30–31) and give yourself a score for each one. Do not try and compare yourself with other people you know. The important thing is for you to determine which of the skill areas are most important for *you*. Use a range of 6 – 1. 6 = 'definite skill'. 1 = 'no skill at all'.

When you have rated yourself against each item, simply add up your scores for each *skill* area. The results should give you some idea of the areas in which your skills are strongest. At this stage it is perhaps tempting to try and relate your *skill* score to various kinds of work, but remember, we have many skills that we use primarily in leisure or non work settings.

There will also be skill areas which the questionnaire has not covered in sufficient detail. Management and leadership skills are not mentioned explicitly. Neither are keyboard and many other manual skills. Scientific investigation and research skills might also have been included. If you feel you have skills which are not mentioned in the checklist, please include them in the **Personal Profile** on page 53. The aim of the exercise is, after all, to stimulate you to identify those skills which *you* think you have.

Example 1
Anyone working in an insurance company, making changes to existing policies, renewals, etc., is likely to need some specific core skills. As well as being able to pay close attention to detail, they will also need communication skills, *in particular when dealing with telephone enquiries from brokers and customers,* numerical skills *for calculating new premiums and insurance rates, the* practical skills *of using calculators and computer keyboards, and the* problem solving skills *involved in dealing with customer enquiries and problems.*

Example 2
Self employed craftspeople producing jewellery, ceramics or sculpture are naturally going to have the necessary creative skills. *But they will also need the repertoire of skills associated with running small businesses. They will need* entrepreneurial skills *in promoting and marketing their work properly and* negotiating skills *in managing employees or agents. A recent survey showed that freelance artists, craftspeople and designers spend more time on business promotion than on their creative work.*

My work values

Our values are largely determined by our life experiences. Different childhood experiences, styles and upbringing, social

Questionnaire Four

MY WORK VALUES

score

6 = most important; 1 = least important

I want a job where . . .

... I can get ahead in my career	*(A)*	...
... I can help people cope better with their lives	*(Su)*	...
... there is a high financial reward	*(E)*	...
... job security is guaranteed	*(Se)*	...
... I can work independently of others	*(I)*	...
... I can do things which involve some risk	*(R)*	...
... I can enjoy high social status	*(P)*	...
... there is quite a bit of travel involved	*(V)*	...
... I can enjoy my place of work	*(En)*	...
... I can do work that is socially useful	*(Su)*	...
... I can develop new ideas or products	*(C)*	...
... there is little work related stress	*(Se)*	...
... people respect me for my position	*(P)*	...
... there is plenty of scope for advancement	*(A)*	...
... there are new challenges and ventures	*(R)*	...
... things are left entirely to my own judgement	*(I)*	...
... there is a pleasant working environment	*(En)*	...
... I am in charge of other people	*(Au)*	...
... I can work as part of a team	*(S)*	...
... I can be creative or inventive	*(C)*	...
... a very good standard of living is possible	*(E)*	...
... there are friendly people around me	*(S)*	...
... there is a lot of variety in what I do	*(V)*	...
... I have the authority to get things done	*(Au)*	...

class, educational influences all contribute to the development of our own value systems. Some people are motivated by a strong sense of achievement. They will look for highly paid, high status jobs, and may thrive in a business environment. Others may look for work which is intrinsically interesting which will, at the same time, meet their need for stability and social contact with other people. Others may need the opportunity to be creative and innovative. Our personal and work values have an important part to play in career planning and decision making.

Our values and needs may change with time. What seemed important to us at one stage in our lives may give way to other concerns. For example, anyone wanting to own a home for the first time may subjugate some of their values to finding a job with sufficiently high pay. Once established in their new home, their needs and value priorities might change again.

Given the choice between a high salary and working in a friendly environment, which would you choose? Would you rather use your talents to the full or go for a job which carried status and prestige? The values questionnaire raises such issues.

Score yourself against each of the statements in Questionnaire Four. A score of 6 denotes values which are *very important* to you, and a score of 1 those which are *unimportant*.

When you have given yourself a score on each of the statements, add up the scores according to the code alongside each item and fill in the Score Sheet opposite. You will find that every statement falls into one of 12 value categories. The score itself is not as important as which values you rank higher than others.

SCORE SHEET

Value	Score
ADVANCEMENT *(A)* Upward mobility and promotion. More interesting work.	☐
SOCIAL *(S)* Friendly contact with workmates. Attending to and talking with people.	☐
ECONOMIC *(E)* High salary and financial rewards.	☐
SECURITY *(Se)* Job stability and regular income. No threat to economic or social well-being.	☐
INDEPENDENCE *(I)* Autonomy – freedom to make decisions and take the initiative.	☐
PRESTIGE *(P)* Being seen in an important role. Social, economic or occupational status.	☐
VARIETY *(V)* Change and variety in task and place of work. The opportunity to train.	☐
ENVIRONMENT *(En)* Pleasant physical surroundings.	☐
SUPPORT *(Su)* Helping people. Work of social or community value.	☐
CREATIVE *(C)* Being original and dealing with new ideas. Creating new products. Finding different solutions to problems.	☐
RISK *(R)* An element of uncertainty. Financial and other kinds of risk.	☐
AUTHORITY *(Au)* Influence and control over other people. Leading others and making decisions.	☐

In Summary:

MY WORK VALUES

The work values which are most significant to me
are . . .

The work values which have a lesser importance
are to do with . . .

The ratings you have given yourself in each of the value categories have something significant to say about the kind of work you will find rewarding. If you found it difficult to distinguish which are the more important values, it suggests that, in any future career, you may have to make trade-offs between certain values. A job providing high prestige and financial rewards might provide a poor working environment. Equally a job in a management hierarchy, giving plenty of opportunity to exercise your authority, might not satisfy your creative values. The checklist, however, should enable you to make a statement about your predominant values. This can go in your **Personal Profile**.

❝DAVID *gave himself scores of 28 and 23 under the* Physical *and* Problem solving *skill headings and 20 for* numeracy. *At the lower end,* language *and* creative *skills scored 10 and 9 respectively. This was also reflected in his sporting interests – he is a keen badminton player – and in his academic interests – geography and environmental science. For David the most important* work values *are to do with* variety (11), indepedence (9) *and* security (8). *Careers under active consideration by David are cartography, land surveying and, his ideal job choice, countryside management.* ❞

Significant influences

As individuals, our life choices and decisions are often shaped by the people around us and also by major events. Family and friends can be powerful influences on career decisions. Was it so surprising that Vanessa, Corin and Lynn Redgrave should all become actors like their father? Perhaps not, because we all recognize so easily the process of 'following in father's footsteps'. There may also be 'significant others' outside the family who influence our lives. Richard Burton, for example ascribed much of his interest in literature and acting to one particular secondary school teacher. The communities in which we are brought up, the educational experiences we have been exposed to, influence and shape our ideas about the kind of people we can become and the nature of our working futures. The two examples amply illustrate this process.

A student describes the background to the early career decision to study accountancy.

'My parents' attitudes worked on me as a subtle form of propaganda from an early age. My father is a chartered accountant and my mother ran her own business. I was brought up to believe that workers in the public sector, in government departments, were feather-bedded and idle; that the only kind of work to consider was professional work in business; the only respectable form of accountancy was chartered accountancy; and that higher education was all very well as long as it led successfully to a suitable job.'

Serendipitous life events helped to determine the nature of this person's first job.

'I was introduced to working with horses almost by accident. One day my father brought home an old pony from the market – a gift to the family. I hadn't expressed any interest in horses before then, but of all the children in the family I was the one who was prepared to get up early to feed and look after it. Later, when I was 12, he bought me another pony, and the Pony Club became a big influence in my life. Later my decision to work full-time with horses came as a result of my wanting to leave home. A local doctor and his wife knew I was keen on riding and told me about the chance of being a working pupil. I went on to become a BHSAI.'

Both of the case studies show the importance of 'significant others' in shaping our career choices.

Try and identify the people and events who have had an influence on your career thinking. Try to recognize whether any future decision you make is wholly yours or whether, in your thinking, you are trying to please someone else. Answering the questions should help.

"By the time I was his age I was reading balance sheets"

© Hector Breeze. Reprinted by kind permission of *Private Eye*.

Questionnaire Five
SIGNIFICANT INFLUENCES

1. How did your family background influence your notion of what work could be?

2. What did your background tell you about jobs which were acceptable or otherwise?

3. What perceptions does your present circle of friends and acquaintances have about work?

4. How has your experience of education shaped your ideas about the kinds and types of work that are acceptable?

My ideal job

Look back over your life. Try and remember the fantasies you had in childhood or later about the kind of person you would like to be, the kind of things you would like to do. Write them down. They can often provide important clues to what you would like to achieve in life and work.

Now try and fantasize about the kind of future you would like to see for yourself, the kind of lifestyle you would like, the kind of work you would like to be doing. On a separate sheet of paper try to draw, paint or describe in words what you would like to do.

Having done that, try and define more precisely the kind of job you would like to be doing.

"Shall we put down 'some form of community service', Bowker?"

From *Caring Professions Casebook.* © 1987 Hobsons Publishing plc.

Questionnaire Six
IN YOUR IDEAL JOB

1. What would you be working at?

2. What kind of people would you be with?

3. How would you describe the work setting?

4. Where would you be living?

5. What would be your rewards?

Work experience

> 'Only a fool claims to learn from experience.'
>
> *Oscar Wilde*

I do not agree with Oscar Wilde. Most people undervalue their contribution at the workplace and fail to recognize the range of skills they have learned and the things they have accomplished. It is only by a thorough review of work experience that you can identify all the things that you can do.

Reviewing work experience can also help you to identify trends in the way you have coped with work. Have you always felt bored after the first few weeks or months in a new job? Have you always tried to innovate and do things differently from your predecessors? Are you capable of coping with sustained pressures? Do you always end up in conflict with your superiors? Do you enjoy working long hours? This kind of analysis provides insights about yourself particularly if discussed with someone you can trust, and who will give honest feedback.

At a practical level, of course, many people who change career build on their previous experience rather than make a fresh start. People in mid career, who suddenly find themselves redundant, may have the option of becoming freelance or self employed, or joining with people with complementary expertise and experience, or they might have taken with them a network of clients and business contacts. Their previous experience is not lost, but used as the basis for a new venture. Most people making changes in mid career will develop skills already acquired rather than ditch them to take on new ones.

WORK AUTOBIOGRAPHY

Using the job you are now doing, or a job you have done in the past, try the following analysis. Describe it as fully as you can, using the following questions as guidelines. Do not attempt to evaluate your performance but, rather, aim to recall everything about the work you did.

1. Describe the **work organization**. Was it large or small? Private company or public sector? What kind of atmosphere did it have?

2. Write about the **job content** in detail. What tasks were involved? What problems or situations did you typically encounter? What

skills did you learn or improve on? What training were you exposed to?

3. How far did it use your **intelligence** and **personality**? What knowledge did you gain?

4. Were there any particular **achievements** you felt proud of? How was success determined? How was your performance monitored?

5. What scope was there for **personal development?**

6. What were the **people** like that you worked with? Were there any particular individuals who helped or considered your personal and career development?

7. What was the effect on your **lifestyle** in terms of working hours and travel-to-work time? What were the implications for your family or partners?

8. Analyse **peak experiences**. Were there times when you felt fulfilled or good about the work you were doing? What characterized these times?

When you have finished your work autobiography, it should be possible to identify aspects of your career you would like to leave behind. Draw up two lists, as shown, with the first list paying particular attention to skills and interests.

My investment in work time

> 'I like work. I can sit and look at it for hours'.
>
> *Jerome K. Jerome*

Japanese managers lose face if they leave their offices before their employees. Many of them will spend long hours at the workplace simply waiting for the workers to go home. 'Yuppy' money market operators have long working hours, often tied to the opening and closing hours of world stock markets. Some of us are less work orientated. For most of us the average day is comprised of a number of elements:

1. *Working or 'sold' time*: which we hire out or use for generating income.

2. *Discretionary or spare time*: which we use for leisure and socializing.

Questionnaire Seven

WORK EXPERIENCE

Things which, on the basis of my work experience, I would like to use in future.	Things which, on the basis of my work experience, I would want to avoid.

3. *Maintenance time*: which we use for sleeping, eating and generally maintaining ourselves.

The more time we spend at work, the more we squeeze the other two. In making a choice of job and career, it is therefore important to be clear about the amount of time we want to invest, so that we can achieve a balance. In addition, the way the working week is structured can vary tremendously from job to job: airline workers, hotel catering staff, nurses and police officers all have to cope with *shift work* of one kind or another. Many office workers, by contrast, are able to enjoy a certain amount of autonomy in the hours they work with *flexitime* arrangements. Many professional workers are expected to work *overtime* without additional salary; other workers will have nationally agreed pay rates for overtime working. As we saw earlier, increasing numbers of jobs are being created on a *part-time* basis at the expense of full-time jobs. The amount of time we want to invest is, therefore, a key element in defining our ideal job.

Allied to the notion of time investment is our whole relationship with work itself. On the one hand some people see their working life as a segment of their lives which intrudes as little as possible on the mainstream of their existence. For others, life is work; consequently, work is a central component of their lifestyle and any distinction between work and leisure is meaningless. How do you view your preferred relationship with work? Try and place yourself somewhere along the continuum on page 46. When you have done that, try and place other people you know at various points on the scale.

A sense of place

Many jobs require *mobility*. Managers of banks or retail companies, members of the armed services, computer consultants and others who work on a contract basis, all have to change location fairly frequently and the choice of where they work is seldom their own. Career advancement will depend on their ability to relocate home and family and adjust to a new setting many times over.

For married women the issue of mobility and careers has often been a vexed one. All too often women have had to try and build their own careers around the job moves of their partners. For the dual career family, and for women in particular, the issue of geography is a major determinant of job and career decisions.

Questionnaire Eight
MY INVESTMENT IN WORK TIME

I couldn't possibly do something I wasn't interested in. There is no difference for me between work and leisure. My life is my work.	Work is an important part of my life and although it is not my sole reason for living, it certainly takes precedence over leisure, entertainment and non work activities.	I want to achieve some kind of balance between the energy I devote to work and that which I devote to non work. Work and leisure are equally important.	Although I work reasonably hard while I am at work, when it comes to 5 p.m. I want to switch off. I refuse to take work home. My own time is very precious to me.	The kind of work I do has very little significance. All I want is the chance to earn enough to have a reasonable social/leisure/ family life.

Which statement would you subscribe to? Write your name in the appropriate space above.
Where would your friends, relatives or acquaintances fit on the chart?

46

Questionnaire Nine

MY JOB LOCATION

	√	X

1. I need a job that fits in with wherever my partner is. ☐ ☐

2. I want a job which takes me abroad/to exciting places. ☐ ☐

3. I am prepared to commute for between an hour and two hours a day. ☐ ☐

4. I will work anywhere as long as the job is interesting. ☐ ☐

5. I want to work within five or ten minutes' travel time from my home. ☐ ☐

6. I want to work from home. ☐ ☐

7. I would be prepared to live in another country on a temporary basis/semi-permanently. ☐ ☐

8. I am content to travel long distances as part of my job. ☐ ☐

9. I would like a job in which . . .

Deciding whether to relocate, or which person's career should take precedence, are increasingly common preoccupations.

At the same time, the availability of jobs in the local travel-to-work area is of vital importance in putting career ideas into practice. Very often the local labour market can be the major determinant in assessing the prospects for returning to work after a career break. For young people living with parents, knowledge of local job opportunities will also be required.

In thinking about where you want to work, try and ally yourself to one or more of the statements on page 47 and, in discounting the others, try and say why they might not be appropriate in your position. Whichever box(es) you tick will have major implications for the later stages of the career planning process: **Exploring, Researching** and **Promoting.** The kind of job vacancy sources you use and the kind of approaches you make to employers will depend on where you are looking for work.

The job interests profile

We all know what interests are. They are the activities we engage in, normally in our spare time, that give us enjoyment and satisfaction. Horse riding or hang-gliding, badminton or bridge, there is an endless range of leisure activities available, given the opportunity. If you have completed Questionnaire Two on page 29, you will already have a statement about your life interests. Now we are moving on to look at something different: your **job interests**.

Read through the 60 items representing different kinds of work activity. Whenever you read something that interests you, even slightly, put a tick by it. It does not really matter whether you think you will be good at the activity concerned, simply register your *interest* in it. Remember you do *not* have to choose one out of each group. You can underline as many or as few as you wish.

Questionnaire Ten
MY JOB INTERESTS

		√
B	Run a restaurant	☐
P	Train sales staff	☐
R	Check pollutant levels in rivers	☐
A	Design textiles	☐
E	Wire a public address system	☐
B	Estimate the value of houses	☐
P	Give speech therapy to children	☐
R	Analyse statistical data	☐
A	Work as a freelance illustrator	☐
E	Test electronic components	☐
B	Manage the catering for a large company	☐
P	Answer travel enquiries and make holiday bookings	☐
R	Design experiments for producing new cell cultures	☐
A	Produce designs for an advertising campaign	☐
E	Plan heating and lighting for offices	☐
B	Interview applicants for clerical/administrative work	☐
P	Provide nursing care for the elderly	☐
R	Test computer systems	☐
A	Report on news for the local media	☐
E	Install radio and television transmitters	☐
B	Check and analyse a company's annual accounts	☐
P	Help young people with educational problems	☐
R	Administer drugs to hospital patients	☐
A	Perform in community arts projects	☐
E	Design steel structures for a petroleum plant	☐
B	Brief a sales team about the launch of a new product	☐
P	Advise on mortgages and personal finance	☐
R	Work on a conservation project	☐
A	Make and sell jewellery	☐
E	Produce drawings for electrical/mechanical equipment	☐

49

		√
B	Calculate insurance premiums	☐
P	Train the young unemployed	☐
R	Plan treatment for patients with limb disorders	☐
A	Design the landscaping for a leisure centre	☐
E	Install bespoke kitchens and bathrooms	☐
B	Advise business clients on computer software	☐
P	Teach in a secondary school or college	☐
R	Develop new health products	☐
A	Restore antique furniture	☐
E	Design and service agricultural machinery	☐
B	Advise companies on financing business loans	☐
P	Supervise and advise people on probation	☐
R	Write technical manuals	☐
A	Carry out freelance press photography	☐
E	Design electronic circuits for flight simulators	☐
B	Plan the shipping of exported goods	☐
P	Work for a community welfare charity	☐
R	Analyse blood samples to detect diseases	☐
A	Edit magazines/books for publication	☐
E	Renovate old buildings	☐
B	Organize tours for foreign tourists	☐
P	Find accommodation for homeless families	☐
R	Work in a forensic science laboratory	☐
A	Commission publicity materials	☐
E	Estimate the costs of building projects	☐
B	Manage the local branch of a building society	☐
P	Organize conferences and exhibitions	☐
R	Carry out seismographic surveys for a mining company	☐
A	Design film and television graphics	☐
E	Service computer hardware	☐

When you have ticked the items that sound interesting, simply add up all the *B* items, *P* items, and so on , and record your total on the Job Interests Profile.

JOB INTERESTS PROFILE

CODE	INTEREST	SCORE
B	Business/Organizing	☐
P	People/Social	☐
R	Research/Scientific	☐
A	Artistic/Creative	☐
E	Engineering/Practical	☐

From the outset, it is important to say that some people may underline 20 or so items, others will indicate an interest in only four or five; but that really does not matter. However many or few items interest you, it should be possible to see a pattern in your replies. Is your score higher for one interest type than another? If so, this could have particular implications for your future career direction. As you can see, each category represents a range of job activities.

The *Business/Organizing* category includes a range of job activities commonly found in business careers from banking to the administrative functions of a manufacturing company.

The *Research/Scientific* category includes a range of scientific activities, broadly defined to include environmental and life sciences.

The *Artistic/Creative* category includes a range of activities associated with the visual arts, media work and design.

In the *Engineering/Practical* category are items mainly to do with the development of manufactured products as well as the testing and maintenance of plant and equipment.

Finally, the *People/Social* category includes a range of job activities concerned with working with or supporting other people in their lives.

When you have entered your scores in the **Job Interests Profile** you may have a key to the kinds of job activity that are going to interest you most. Alternatively you may find that there is no particular pattern; that no one interest category predominates. No matter. Simply review the items you have under lined. There may be some key words that you have responded to, which become clear at a second glance. Failing that, ask a friend to review your **Job Interests Profile** with you. They will be able to ask you about your replies.

Finally it is important to repeat: this profile will only summarize what you are interested in. It cannot predict what you are likely to be good at.

The case study illustrates how the process of designing a personal profile can help in prompting a successful career change.

❛LISA *had a good honours degree in English. Her main career idea had always been teaching, but family and friends had deterred her. Having followed her husband's job moves, she got a job in educational administration. She was very successful but regretted an earlier decision not to go into personnel work.*

After working hard and not getting a regrading she now felt it was time to make a decision about her career direction – one that she would make for herself and therefore be happy with.

She still toyed with the idea of training to teach but was also considering a job in industry in either personnel or training. What should she do?

From her values statement it was clear that prestige and advancement were going to be key factors. In terms of skills, Lisa gave herself high scores for influencing, reporting and social skills, but lower ratings for creative, problem-solving and numerical skills. Her job interests were largely in the business/organizing category but also in the people/social category.

And the outcome: Lisa started applying for jobs in commerce and fairly quickly found a job in a prestigious multinational finance company, where she reported to senior management on the implementation of their business systems. ❜

Having completed the exercises, you should now be able to summarize your findings from each of the completed question-naires. This is the basis of your **Personal and Career Profile**.

Simply gather your replies from all ten questionnaires and fill in the summary form. You will need this later on.

My Personal and Career Profile

Q.1 My achievements have been . . .

Q.2 My interests include . . .

Q.3 My skills are . . .

Q.4 My work values concern . . .

Q.5 Significant influences have been . . .

Q.6 My ideal job would be . . .

Q.7 My work experience has included . . .

Q.8 My investment in work time is . . .

Q.9 Geographical considerations include . . .

Q.10 My job interests appear to be . . .

PART 3

LOOKING FOR IDEAS

▼ Compiling your options list
▼ Job Analysis
▼ Job Study
▼ Design your own job
▼ The self development option

What options do I have? What is open to me? These are typical questions. Before committing themselves, people want to see something of the big picture – the range of things they could consider. The **Explorer** stage of the career planning process, concerned with generating a list of possible options, together with the **Researcher** stage, to do with a detailed investigation of each idea, are the most time consuming. You will need some important career planning skills:

★ **Creativity** in identifying alternative career options and drawing up a list of ideas

★ **Making contact** with friends, colleagues and other people in work to provide you with information and advice

★ **Information research** to find out as much as you can about the various options you have identified

★ **Evaluating and decision making** – choosing which career ideas to take further and which to put on hold for the present or reject completely.

This chapter is all about making an options list – one, two or more career options that you would like to consider and then research in some depth. You may already have one or two ideas at the back of your mind – notions that you have been nurturing for some time and that you now want to explore further. Alternatively, you may be stuck for ideas or perhaps know vaguely what you might like to do, but are not sure whether it could form part of a job.

Compiling your options list

- There is now a lot of *computer software* designed to help people identify career options: CASCAID, JIIG-CAL, PROSPECT and CAREER BUILDER are all computer programmes designed particularly for young people at school and college. You are asked questions about your interests and on the basis of your answers a list of suitable job titles is provided.

- The *Information Sources* at the back of the book are an invaluable source of information on different job and career options.

- *National and local press* provide an important source of job ideas arising from the job vacancies they advertise, as do *trade and* professional journals. A number of the national daily newspapers have job or career columns which provide up-to-date information on a wide variety of occupations. Magazines often feature profiles of career changers and the job market for their readers.

- *Everyone you know* is a potential source of job and career ideas. Friends and family are obvious resources on which to draw. Work colleagues past and present, business contacts, fellow members of clubs and societies can all help to generate ideas, providing you are prepared to allow them into your confidence.

Some of the ideas on your option list will, of course, be tentative, others more concrete. You may want to list options other than jobs: ideas for self employment, courses of education and training, or thoughts on working from home.

Having generated a list of possible career options, what next? The next crucial step is to research them fully. You will know of people who have started a new job only to find that it wasn't what they expected. For them it was a risk, a shot in the dark. But it need not be. A vital task is to test the reality of your ideas. This means researching your ideas from written sources and then going one stage further – analysing what the job or career is like in *real life* to find out exactly what is involved. Is chartered accountancy boring? Is working in the media glamorous? Investigating the reality of careers and jobs which interest you should enable you to avoid stereotypes and gain an accurate impression on which to base your career plans. Two simple exercises **Job Analysis** and **Job Study** will help you distinguish fact from fiction, reality from the glossy image.

Job Analysis

One way of finding out more about a job is to do what is called a **Job Analysis**. Personnel officers often get involved in this kind of exercise. They observe or interview an employee in order to write a job description which they can then use as a basis for selecting applicants for a similar job. You can do the same thing, but using printed sources of information. Take an example of the kind of work you would like to do and using job adverts, publicity material and careers reference books, list the essential activities involved in the job.

When you have completed this simple analysis you can then list the kind of skills that might be involved. A recording engineer, for example, as well as perfect hearing, might be expected to have effective communication skills, technical and problem solving skills, some musical ability, a knowledge of basic electronics and different kinds of stereo system, as well as the capacity to work under stress.

EXAMPLE

Job Analysis: Banking Assistant

ACTIVITIES	SKILLS INVOLVED
Inputting details of transactions at a computer terminal	Keyboard skills Visual perception
Checking customer transactions	Attention to detail
Ensuring the Branch balances at the end of the day	Numerical skills
Answering customer queries	Problem solving, social skills and relating to people

The **Job Analysis** checklist invites you to look at a range of job features including entry qualifications, relevant work experience and likely rewards. When you analyse the job in this way you can then begin to see how far you measure up to the specification. Take your **Personal and Career Profile** and compare it with the job in question.

Researching a number of different jobs in this way will help you clarify your thinking. It will enable you to reject some ideas and advance others. Relying on the printed word, however, does have its limitations. It could be, for example, that there is considerable variation in the kinds of job/work you are researching. There could be informal entry points or short cuts that may not be evident and so you need to make a more detailed assessment. This is where **Job Study** comes in.

You can now turn your attention to a wider range of questions connected with the job you are researching.

JOB ANALYSIS

Job Title		**Me**
What skills does the job require?	➡	What skills do I have?
What work experience, if any, is necessary?	➡	What experience do I have?
What education and training is necessary?	➡	What education and training do I have?
What physical and/or personal qualities are important?	➡	What physical and/or personal qualities do I want to put to use?
What interests does the job call for?	➡	Which of my interests would the job tap?
What would the job give me (for example, pay, conditions, prospects)?	➡	What work values and needs do I have?
What future prospects are there for this type of work in a given geographical location?	➡	Where do I want to work?
What other demands would the job make (eg travel, long hours)?	➡	How would this job affect my circumstances, domestic commitments, etc.?

Job Study

Researching one job in detail

Most of us feel reluctant to contact employers for information about jobs and vacancies (except in response to specific adverts). It could be seen to be canvassing for ourselves – something that 'isn't quite cricket'. And yet, as shown in the next section canvassing is all important in letting employers know that you are available and actively looking for work. In the process of career choice and planning, what we often need is more information before making an application. School students on work experience, degree and higher diploma students undertaking sandwich course placements, and people doing temporary work, have the ideal opportunity to observe a particular job at first hand – to be exposed to all that the job has to offer. They can test the reality of the work involved and in doing so can decide whether they will be suited to it.

There is a method of researching opportunities in more detail that anyone can use. It is called **Job Study**. When you have decided on one career option that you would like to research in detail:

▶ find someone who is doing what you want to do

▶ ask to see them for an advisory interview and arrange a time

▶ take along a notebook and pen

▶ use the **Job study interview** checklist as a rough guide when asking questions.

Most people enjoy being asked to describe their jobs and are usually only too willing to talk, particularly if you can find a time when they are least busy. For students it is very easy to approach employing organizations with the explanation that you are completing a project or assignment. If you want to be really professional you can take along a tape recorder and ask to record the interview.

JOB STUDY INTERVIEW

Use these questions when interviewing people in paid employment.
If you are talking to people who are self employed you will have to amend the questions accordingly.

Main responsibilities
★ What is your job title?

★ What is involved in your job?

★ What kinds of abilities, skills, personal qualities are required to do it successfully?

Selection and training
★ What qualifications are required?

★ How are people recruited?

★ What selection procedures are used?

★ What training is given?

★ How would you assess the training given?

Conditions and rewards
★ What demands does the job make outside 'normal' working hours?

★ How does it affect your lifestyle?

★ What pressures are there?

★ What sort of financial prospects and fringe benefits does the job offer?

★ What are the personal rewards from a job like this?

★ What are the negative aspects?

Career development
★ How is your work performance appraised?

★ What prospects for advancement are there within this job?

★ How easy is it to develop your career elsewhere?

Possible changes
★ What changes are taking place in this kind of work?

★ What is the likely impact of new technology?

★ What advice would you give to anyone coming in to a job like this?

61

Handling the job study interview

For anyone without experience of interviewing, approaching a complete stranger to ask about their work can be daunting. Here are some suggestions about the way to conduct your 'information' or advisory interview.

▶ *Be clear about your intentions* when contacting the person you wish to interview. Explain that the information given is for your own personal use to help in your career planning.

▶ *Negotiate the amount of time* it will take. Thirty minutes should be adequate, if that is all they can spare.

▶ *Be friendly.* Let the other person talk as much as possible by using open-ended questions, such as 'What do you like about your job?' Open-ended questions begin with 'How?' 'What?' 'Why?'.

▶ *Do not bombard anyone with questions.* They should not feel they are being interrogated. Let the interview roam freely. You may not get all your questions answered, and you may have to accept this.

▶ *Ask permission* to take notes, or, if you have the technology, tape record the interview, but only with prior permission.

▶ *Finally, thank them* for their time and ask if they can refer you to any other information sources or contacts that might prove useful.

When you have completed your **Job Study** interview, it may help to write it up as a report, which you can keep and refer to. Now you should have a far clearer idea of what is involved in the job you have been considering. You will have made at least one personal contact, and your notes will be useful in making any further applications, or as an *aide-mémoire* when you go for selection interviews. Finally, you should have a sense of whether this is a job that you would like to do.

Design your own job

Having looked at a number of possible career options and perhaps researched one type of work in depth, you should now be in a

Questionnaire Eleven

DESIGN YOUR OWN JOB

1. What would you like to be doing on a day-to-day basis?

2. Which of your skills would you want the job to tap?

3. What rewards would you be looking for?

4. What kind of people would you like to work with?

5. What sort of organization would you prefer to work for?

position to design your own job. Using the outline on page 63 and referring back to the **Job Analysis** and **Job Study**, compose a description of the kind of work you are looking for. Be clear about the job content, the things you would like to do and the tasks that might be involved. Determine which of your skills you would like to use, the needs that the job might meet, the work values that it could help you express. Think carefully about the knowledge you have gained from previous work experience. How much of this would you want to use? Be specific about the rewards you would like. In sum, this should be a more concrete statement of your ideas than the *Ideal Job* outline you completed as part of your **Personal and Career Profile**.

The result, your Job Design, could form the basis of your marketing approaching to potential employers and prepare you for the next stage of the career planning process.

Most of the examples listed so far have been to do with jobs. But not everyone will include full-time or even part-time paid employment on their options list. For women wanting to return to earning after a career break, the options might include various types of contract or home work, or retraining for new skills and confidence building. The contact making and information research skills mentioned earlier will be important, however.

If you are unemployed and live in an area of high unemployment it could be that some of the Government's special measures, for example, Employment Training provide options to be considered. Alternatively you may be in a position to look at some of the options described in *Information Sources* on p. 95.

"As a matter of fact it started as a holiday job."

© Hector Breeze. Reprinted by kind permission.

The self development option

If you are already in work and feeling like a career change, it could be that other options exist apart from leaving one job to start another. As we saw in an earlier chapter, it is perfectly possible to develop other leisure/work interests in addition to holding down a full-time job. Many opportunities for self employment develop from hobbies or other interests, which are nurtured and developed over a number of years.

Alternatively, it could be that self development in your present job is more of a viable proposition. Changing oneself and living with the job is sometimes a preferred alternative, particularly when there are family or other constraints which prevent an immediate change of job location.

One obvious option is to consider opportunities for **training or retraining**. Training comes in many different forms. Informal or on-the-job training occurs all the time, but many companies offer their own *in-company courses and training programmes.* In developing technical skills, employers may well request training from equipment manufacturers or suppliers. Often they will use commercial training organizations. Employees may also be allowed to follow part-time courses at local colleges or polytechnics on a *day release* basis. Even if employers do not offer a time allowance for training, they may well help with fees.

It has to be acknowledged, however, that training and retraining is not a reality for most of the working population. Companies in this country have a poor record on this count and therefore negotiation of time for study and training may well prove difficult. At the very least, companies should be able to give you some support for self study courses in your own time.

Often training and access to it will be just one aspect of a company's staff development. Some large companies will have a *career development plan* for professional staff, which ensures that individuals can progress from one job to another within the company. This is particularly the case when organizations find recruitment difficult and want to retain as many staff as possible. The name given to this process is usually *'career management'* or *'staff development'*. It is often implemented by a personnel or staff manager whose job it is to monitor the progress of individuals through the organization. It usually entails an *appraisal interview* between the employee and manager to review performance, strengths and weaknesses, identify particular skills and set career objectives. The recommended outcome of the appraisal is then acted upon by the company and the individual's path is charted.

Another method used for the development of senior managers is the *assessment centre* or *development workshop* which takes place over one or more days. Managers are asked to carry out specific tasks, or complete a psychological testing procedure. Results are then fed back to the workshop participants and used as a basis for training and future assignments and gradings.

Some companies recruit staff at mainly one level. The computer systems house, CAP, mainly recruits graduates; 70 to 80 per cent of its total staff have degrees and some 65 per cent started with the company as graduate trainees. With an active policy of training and career management, the company tries to develop the careers of its trainees along one of two main routes: project management or technical consultancy. Most management jobs in the company will therefore go to 'home-grown' managers chosen from the company's existing employees.

In many organizations, *staff appraisal interviews* take place on a regular, annual basis. Staff sit down with their supervisor or departmental manager to review progress and job performance, to identify areas of possible improvement and development and to look at training needs. Often staff will have a written copy of the appraisal so that both parties know what has been agreed in the way of action. The appraisal will then form the basis of any future promotion or career development.

The further study option

After exploring some of your job ideas in depth you may well find that what you want to do calls for further education or training. Alternatively, you may simply want to improve your qualification level before re-entering the job market. It could be that retraining on a part-time basis will be one way of securing a change to a better job. Whatever your position, the following exercise in course design could help you to specify exactly what you want from a course of study. You can then look through the course directories to see whether the kind of course you want actually exists.

Think carefully about the kind of course you might want to do. Consider the implications in terms of what you might have to invest in time and money, and summarize the likely rewards in terms of skills, qualifications, opportunities for personal development. The questionnaire provides a framework.

Questionnaire Twelve
DESIGN YOUR OWN COURSE

1. What subjects would you like to study? What would interest you?

2. How much time are you prepared to invest?

3. Will it be full-time or part-time?

4. Do you want it to be job related? Or related to your own development?

5. What are the financial implications?

6. What entry qualifications can you offer?

7. Are there any geographical considerations?

Having designed your course of study, you may well find that access to it depends on your present qualification level. Most students leaving school will know that there is a well trodden path from GCSE to A levels to degree or higher diploma course or, alternatively, from GCSE to vocational qualification such as BTEC (Business and Technical Education Council) or CGLI (City and Guilds of London Institute). The qualifications chart attempts to simplify the range of different qualifications which exist.

Where can you study? If you are thinking of retraining or studying for additional qualifications, your first point of reference could be your local *college of further education*. As well as providing a range of nationally recognized full-time courses in subjects such as business studies, engineering or secretarial studies, they will also provide part-time courses to prepare you for the examinations of various professional bodies, e.g. marketing, surveying or banking. The colleges cater for people of all ages and a wide variety of educational backgrounds providing a focus for 'recreational' courses such as car maintenance or conversational Spanish but, more importantly, provide courses leading to formal qualifications such as GCSE, A levels, BTEC diplomas and City and Guilds qualifications. If you want to study at a higher level or qualify professionally by full-time study, it is more likely that your course will be in a *polytechnic* or a *university*, which offer three or four year degree courses in a wide range of subjects. Polytechnics provide a range of courses at higher diploma as well as degree level and offer a range of options for part-time study. Universities provide the majority of postgraduate courses in the UK. Both polytechnics and universities require well defined entry qualifications and usually set grades at A level.

It is important to remember, however, that there are now courses designed particularly for adults, which may not require qualifications for entry. 'Return to Learning' or 'Working Opportunities for Women' (WOW) courses provide women returners with specific skills to help them re-enter the job market. 'Fresh Start' courses exist for any adults who may have left school without formal qualifications. 'Access' courses related to a specific subject, for example, humanities, computing or construction, provide a foundation course designed to prepare students for study in higher education. The books and course directories mentioned in *Information Sources* will provide you with more information. Your local educational guidance service will also be an important first point of contact.

In addition, there are other courses for adults already in work. For those who want to update their skills, there are a range of short courses under the Department of Education and Science PICKUP programme (Professional, Industrial and Commercial Updating). At the same time 'distance' learning is becoming more available for those who live in rural areas or for whom attendance at classes is impractical. The Open College provides this kind of opportunity, as does the Open University. The breadth and range of education and training provision has been extended to give more adults the opportunity for further study.

In addition to the colleges mentioned above there are also other venues, particularly for skill training. On the one hand, government training centres provide courses mainly geared to industrial needs and the local job market; on the other, a range of private organizations offer short, specialized courses, e.g. beauty therapy, complementary medicine.

Your review of qualification and training routes completed, you should then be in a position to decide on the kind of investment you want to make to help you in your career or job change.

THE QUALIFICATIONS MAZE

Some of the Main Educational Qualifications

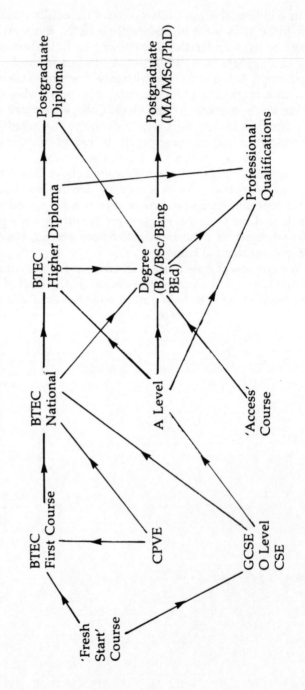

PART 4

MARKETING YOURSELF

▼ Target your employers
▼ Develop a personal network
▼ Find your own mentor
▼ Go to a job hunting seminar
▼ Get professional help
▼ Put yourself on paper
▼ Prepare for an interview
▼ The interview outcome

When you have singled out one or two ideas for work or future training, the next stage is to put them into practice. This is the **Promoter** stage of the career planning process which is about self marketing, convincing other people that you are the right person for the job, or a suitable candidate for a course of study or training. The following discussion is primarily concerned with the theme of job search, but many of the methods suggested apply to other forms of the selection process, for example, applying for a course of study.

The first step is comparatively simple. List all the facts about yourself that a potential employer is going to want to know:

★ some basic biographical information – your date of birth, nationality, etc.

★ your educational experience – the schools and colleges you have attended, any qualifications gained.

★ your work experience: job titles, employers' names and addresses, the dates you started and left your previous jobs.

★ the tasks you performed in each job, and particular achievements or special projects that may be relevant.

★ what you have to offer a potential employer – your work interests, your personal and social skills.

Taken together with your **Personal and Career Profile** you will now have all the information you need to form the basis of your self presentation. Your written job hunt file will be used to complete application forms and compile a curriculum vitae (see pages 79-80).

Target your employers

The next stage of the marketing process is to decide on your market and to identify organizations which are likely to employ you. Why do you never see the job of bank manager advertised in the press? It is because the clearing banks fill all their management vacancies by the internal promotion of existing staff and their own management development programmes. It has been estimated that something like two-thirds of all jobs are never advertised either because they are filled internally or because they are handled by recruitment agencies. This is why it is a good idea to take an active part in promoting yourself to local companies – there may be more vacancies than you imagine.

At the same time, this process of market research can add a note of realism to your job applications. For example your research of local employment opportunities will help you to establish the kind of job vacancies which are likely to occur in your own or preferred geographical area.

You can build up a dossier on likely firms by scanning newspaper ads and looking at journals and magazines. You will soon get to know the kinds of vacancy that occur frequently with particular employers. In addition, you can use the reference sources mentioned in *Information Sources*, or even the Yellow Pages. Your local reference library will have many of the specialist reference books which give lists of companies in a particular business, for example, *The Computer User's Yearbook* or *Travel Trade Directory*. Many professional bodies will have directories of member firms that you can consult. (Some even have their own job vacancy or appointments circulars available to members.)

When you have your list of potential employers, your next step is to decide on whom to target within an organization. Should you write to the personnel officer or to someone else? Many small companies will not have a specific personnel officer, so letters can be sent to the managing director or senior partner. In many medium to large companies, particularly in manufacturing, there will be an established structure of specialist departments as the chart indicates. You might decide to target your application at one of the departmental managers rather than the 'Head of Personnel'.

A MANUFACTURING COMPANY

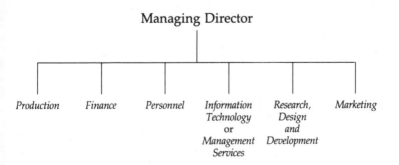

If you have specialist knowledge which you know will be sought after by just one or two companies, it may well be worthwhile to target technical management in a particular company, rather than address your application to the 'Personnel Manager'. In any case it is important to address your application to a **named individual** within the organization.

At the same time as you are researching companies and targeting employers, there are several other steps you can take to help with your self promotion and marketing.

Develop a personal network

How many times have you heard the cliché: 'It's not what you know, but whom you know'? It applies across the job market and is a well recognized phenomenon. Friends, relatives and business contacts are valuable sources of career ideas and information about job opportunities. Building and developing a network of people you can refer to is very important.

The benefits of networking are twofold. First, you can use your personal network to find out about job opportunities which are likely to occur in future and so be ready to apply immediately a vacancy occurs. Second, you may not even need to make a job application. People in your network will be aware that you are looking for a job change and may therefore offer you a job because they know you are available.

You may be thinking that you do not have any contacts to exploit. Perhaps this is something to work on. There are very few rules involved. You simply have to talk to people and, if you like, make some of your plans and ideas known to them, and find out whether they have contacts which may prove useful to you. You can develop contacts by joining clubs, professional associations or societies, going to further or adult education classes, doing voluntary work, or getting involved in any form of community activity. The next important step is to keep a mental or written record of the contacts you have made.

Find your own mentor

A recent management development technique is to put a relatively junior manager under the wing of a middle or senior manager, to gain advice and to increase the protégé's experience and business ability. It is called *mentoring*. In addition to giving a guide to work performance, the mentor also helps the junior manager to have a clearer sense of career direction. Career aspirations can often be turned into realistic objectives, because the senior partner can ensure that the junior manager gets the right degree of exposure in the organization and put him or her forward for promotion.

If you are already in work, there may well be someone who can fulfil this role for you, perhaps a departmental manager or immediate supervisor. Even if you are not in work and not in management, it is certainly worth trying to find someone who can be your sponsor or mentor in changing jobs or career. The advantages are obvious. The insights that the older, more experienced person can bring will be of value, as will the contacts in their own personal network. Most people are only too willing to take on this role. They like to be seen as helpful and, in particular, like being told they are experts.

Go to a job hunting seminar

Students about to leave full-time education should have easy access to talks, lectures and seminars on making job applications and going for interviews. For those both in and out of work, job hunting seminars are provided by the Professional and Executive Recruitment (PER) as well as by private agencies. Typically, they will invite you to appraise your skills and experience, assess the local job market and the skills that are required, and then help you to prepare a curriculum vitae and suggest ways of approaching the selection interview. The obvious benefit of attending a course or seminar is the potential for learning from other people's experience.

For anyone who has been unemployed for some time, attendance at a Job Club could well provide a similar opportunity to gain confidence in approaching employers and brushing up your job search skills. Job Clubs also provide typing, copying and telephone facilities and regular support over a number of weeks.

Get professional help

You may be fairly successful at promoting yourself, but you might still want to seek professional help if you are entering a specialized job market and encountering continued rejection. It could be a good idea if you simply want to see what is on offer as part of your job search. As well as the government offices of the Department of Employment – the Job Centres – and offices of the Professional and Executive Recruitment (PER), there are private agencies that help job seekers. Recruitment consultants are paid by employers to provide them with a shortlist of suitable applicants. There is usually no charge to individual candidates. Careers counselling agencies will not only offer to test your suitability for certain careers, they will also help you package yourself more effectively, by designing your job applications or curriculum vitae.

In using any agency there are some important caveats:

★ **Be selective.** Make sure you know exactly what kind of service you are paying for and, if possible, get recommendations from previous clients. In the case of careers counselling agencies, it is worth checking that the staff are professionally trained psychologists. If agencies are also dealing directly with companies in providing careers counselling to employees – something that is called 'outplacement' – you can assume that the agency has some status and standing.

★ **Be assertive.** Be clear about your own needs and brief the agency accordingly. Ask questions about the way they operate. If you place yourself in their hands, do keep in touch with them to check on progress.

A list of the different kinds of recruitment and careers consultancy is provided in the section, *Placement and Helping Agencies* (p. 97).

For young people who are leaving education, the main guidance and placement agency will be the local authority careers service. Careers officers will provide individual careers counselling and give advice on job search, as well as place people in training and jobs.

Put yourself on paper

Traditionally, there are two ways of making written job applications: using a curriculum vitae and completing an application form. Which you use generally depends on the employer's selection process.

The curriculum vitae

This is essentially a career history, a printed summary of your biographical information, education record and work experience. It is a simple and effective way of marketing yourself to an employer. Its task is to secure a job interview, and it is particularly useful when

(a) you are writing speculatively to an employer to ask if they have a job vacancy in your field

(b) the company does not have its own printed application form

(c) the advert states 'please apply in writing to . . . '

The curriculum vitae also has uses outside the process of job hunting – when applying to a bank manager for business finance or when presenting your credentials in non-work settings.

Each curriculum vitae is unique to the individual concerned, but there are, nevertheless, useful guidelines to follow in preparing one. As the example shows, there is a structure which divides up the information into a number of sections. Use your **Personal and Career Profile** and your work experience record to set out information in the following order:

1. **Biographical data:** name, address, telephone number; date of birth, citizenship/nationality.

2. **Education:** Secondary schools or colleges attended with dates, examintion passes with grades, higher education experience, degree or diploma results with a one-line description of the course.

3. **Work experience** (starting with your most recent job): names and details of companies, dates of employment, details of job titles, duties or responsibilities (pinpointing relevant skills and experience).

4. **Further information:** leisure interests, special achievements (work and non-work), additional skills (for example, languages).

5. **Referees:** the names, titles and addresses of at least two people to whom reference can be made.

In addition you should note:

★ *Visual presentation* is vitally important. Your c.v. should look good. Have it professionally typed or compiled on a word processor. Use good quality paper. Set it out so that it is easy to read.

★ *Length:* opinions vary about how long it should be. For anyone with work experience, one side of A4 will patently not suffice. If you include a statement of career aims this will lengthen the c.v. still further.

★ Give a *positive impression* in what you write. One-word descriptions of interests are unhelpful. You need to highlight your achievements in attractive but not flowery prose. If you can, be both succinct and engaging.

The example provided follows a standard format. You may, however, wish to customize your c.v. and design it with one particular employer in mind. In this case, there are additional sections you can include. It is often acceptable to include a statement of your *career plans* and intentions, and this can be particularly appropriate if you are sure that the prospective employer can offer what you are looking for. It is legitimate to have a general section on *achievements*, pointing out any particular success you have had in work, leisure or related fields. Alternatively, under each job heading and list of responsibilities, you could describe the things you have achieved: business success, targets achieved, special awards, promotion, regrading, or projects implemented.

One way of tailoring your application to individual employers is to send an *accompanying letter* with your c.v. Ideally, this should be handwritten in ink on good quality writing paper, and, if possible, addressed to a named person, rather than 'Dear Sir or Madam'. Your covering letter should mention the vacancy or type of work you are applying for and refer to your present employment or course of study. You can then start to refer to information on your c.v. 'As you can see from my curriculum vitae, I have . . . '. More importantly, your letter might also explain or enlarge on the facts presented in your c.v. You can point to directly relevant experience, mention the job areas for which you feel suited or emphasize the contribution you could make to the organization. Your letter could also refer to your present career intentions or reason for the application, for

CURRICULUM VITAE

NAME: Patricia Smith

ADDRESS: 10 Fircroft Road   TELEPHONE: (0802) 236
                    Greenside
                    HA5 2WN

DATE OF BIRTH: 20 November 1962

NATIONALITY: British

EDUCATION AND QUALIFICATIONS

1974-81   Greenside High School

                    GCE O Levels: (6)
                    GCE A Levels: Economics D
                                  Geography D

1981-83   Midlands Polytechnic

                    BTEC Higher Diploma Business Studies
                    (Distinction)

1983-84   Growmore College of Higher Education

                    Postgraduate Diploma:
                    Personnel Management and Industrial
                    Relations

WORK EXPERIENCE

November 1986   Marksman Financial Serivces
to present   Personnel Officer

Duties: Responsible for the full range of
                    personnel services including the
                    implementation of employment legislation,
                    disciplinary and grievance procedures.

                    Recruitment and selection of all staff
                    up to senior manager status.

	Advising on salaries, benefits and grading structure.
	Also responsible for new staff induction in a company with a total staff of 260.
September 1984 to October 1986	District of Blankside Personnel Assistant
Duties:	Responsible for salary administration.
	Administration of pensions and benefits.
	Monitoring staff welfare provision.
June–September 1982	Exchange student working for an accountancy firm in Hanover, West Germany.

FURTHER INFORMATION

I enjoy water sports and belong to a local sub-aqua club.
I have a good working knowledge of German, which I have
developed from several holidays abroad and as an exchange
student at college. I have a clean driving licence.

REFEREES

Oliver Sackton
Managing Director
Marksman Financial Services
2 Bit Road
Easefield
ET3 7RZ

Tel: (Easefield) 3587

John Fowlds
Principal Personnel
  Assistant
Blankside District
  Council
Humbler Road
Blankside
HR7 6PU

Tel: (Blankside) 684382

example: 'My present company is relocating in six months time and I would like to continue working in this geographical area'.

A further way of approaching employers is to provide what the Americans call a *résumé*. This is a curriculum vitae but in a narrative style. Under each point of your education, experience or work record describe the kinds of task performed, providing a full description of what was involved in each job.

The application form

Many people find form filling a drudge. They see it as a boring, though necessary, precursor to an interview. And this is part of the problem. Some company application forms are difficult to complete because of the way they are designed, others because they really attempt to tax the applicants' ingenuity by asking some very awkward questions. Yet most companies will select for interview less than half of all applicants and it is for this reason that application forms *must be taken seriously*. Take time over their completion and you will find that you can create a positive impression in what is, after all, a very competitive situation.

The following guidelines will help you through the first stage of the selection process and (hopefully) gain you an interview.

▶ When you receive your application form, *don't rush to fill it in*. Read it carefully from start to finish. If it is a long and detailed questionnaire, take a photocopy and use the copy to do a draft reply. Some questions will be more open-ended. Look at the job description or company brochure and assess exactly what they are looking for. How far is the application form designed to contain all you have to say about yourself?

▶ *Answer all the questions*, either on your photocopy or on a rough sheet. If there is insufficient space, add additional pages of your own to include with the application form.

▶ *Complete every question*. Don't leave blank spaces.
Pay attention to the visual effect and neatness of your presentation.

▶ You can be rejected for poor spelling so make sure your answers contain *no spelling errors*.

▶ *Write legibly* in dark ink. If your handwriting is untidy, use block capitals or have your answers typed.

▶ Recruiters are trained to spot gaps or discrepancies in your study or employment record, so ensure that you *account fully for your past career*.

▶ In answering open-ended questions write to *create a positive impression*. Never use one word answers. Under 'Interests' for example, never simply answer 'Reading'. Most people read. Describe the kind of things you read and how often.

▶ *Pay attention to your use of language*. Avoid slang and hackneyed phrases. Use clear and simple sentences to create a direct and positive impression.

The job description or company brochure will give you some clues as to what the recruiter is looking for. In a management role, for example, evidence of team leadership skills will be important. Be sure to *highlight your statements* accordingly.

▶ When you have completed the application form, *ask a friend to go over it* in detail, bearing in mind all the points listed above.

▶ When you finish the final version, *take a photocopy*, so that you have a record of everything you have told the employer. Your replies could well form the basis of your selection interview.

Biodata

Some companies have to process thousands of job applications for one particular kind of work. Airlines, for example, receive this number of applications for cabin crew vacancies and personnel staff have to process them as speedily as possible. To cope with this they have begun to use *Biodata*, or more precisely, objectively scored application forms, which are more like questionnaires than open-ended application forms.

To develop a Biodata form, a company will analyse, in detail, a particular job to ascertain the skills and qualifications and to identify the important personality factors required to do it. Then, from their existing staff, they develop a profile of the successful job performer and, finally, design an appropriate application form. Users of Biodata claim that it not only saves time in assessing applications, but also reduces error and possible prejudice. From the applicant's point of view, it produces particular problems. The first example, which refers to qualifications, shows how difficult it can be to explain or fully describe your exam performance when you are simply given a box to tick.

Example 1	**Example 2**

Example 1	**Example 2**
How many separate subjects have you taken at O level/ GCSE?	Which of these qualities has proved to be of most use in your life?

(a) None ☐   *(a)* Capacity for hard work ☐

(b) 1–3 ☐   *(b)* Creativity, originality ☐

(c) 4–6 ☐   *(c)* Getting on with people ☐

(d) 7–9 ☐   *(d)* Self confidence ☐

(e) 10 or more ☐   *(e)* Willingness to take risk ☐

                                  (f) Careful attention to detail ☐

Whilst Biodata forms are generally used to gain factual information about applicants, they may also try to elicit statements about an applicant's personality or values. In the second example, it is difficult for the applicant to know which answer the employer is likely to prefer – a feature of many Biodata forms.

As there is little chance of knowing which of the replies is right or wrong from the employer's point of view, it is largely a question of answering as truthfully as you can. One of the positive outcomes of the use of Biodata forms is that they are more reliable than many other selection methods in making a suitable match between the applicant and the job in question. Second, they are less likely to be discriminatory, since they do not ask questions about marital status, age or ethnic group.

Prepare for an interview

The interview remains the most commonly used method of selecting people for jobs at all levels. This is despite the fact that it is notoriously unreliable from the selector's point of view and is often a poor predictor of future job performance. But it is a method with which more people feel comfortable.

A dictionary definition of the word 'interview' suggests an exchange of ideas, a discussion rather than an interrogation. It is unusual, however, to find a selection interview which takes the form of a relaxed conversation. Typically, the interview consists of a dialogue between interviewer and interviewee in which the interviewer asks most of the questions, whilst the interviewee tries to answer. It is a polite form of interrogation, with an etiquette of its own.

In an ideal interview, the candidate talks for 60 per cent of the time and the interviewer for 40 per cent. The hallmark of poor interviewers is that they talk too much and fail to ask the right questions. If you find that you are faced with an interviewer who does 90 per cent of the talking, you will soon begin to wonder how they are going to be able to make a decision about your potential as an employee – and you will be right. On the other hand, a trained interviewer will be able to make you feel at ease and, by asking questions in the right way, get you talking easily and fluently about your application. From the candidate's point of view, it is very much the luck of the draw which you encounter.

What kinds of interview are there?

For many jobs, candidates are interviewed just once, probably by a personnel officer or line manager. The *one-to-one* interview with one person asking questions of each candidate in turn is the commonest form. It can last from 20 minutes to one hour depending on the level and complexity of the job in question. There are, however, other forms of interview. A *panel* interview is commonly used in education, local government and the Civil Service. Candidates are interviewed by a panel of three or even more people representing different interests or departments, each following their own particular line of questioning. (A glorious example of a panel interview occurs in an early Peter Sellers' film, *Only Two Can Play* in which Sellers is up for the job of town librarian and is interviewed by the entire town council.)

For many senior jobs in an organization – from trainee manager upwards – there may be a first interview with a personnel interviewer followed by second or even third interviews with line managers or perhaps even board directors. The second and third interviews may be of a technical nature and, almost certainly, will represent a narrowing down of the field of candidates. In many instances the first interview is followed by an *assessment centre*, of which more later.

Be your natural self – as far as possible – but still acknowledge the formality of the interview. As it is so difficult to predict what is going to happen, the keynote is sensitivity. Try and be as aware as possible of what is going on around you so that you can respond accordingly. Interview success depends, too, on the extent of your preparation. Getting yourself in the right frame of mind is all important; so too is finding out as much as you can about the employer. One useful method of preparing yourself is to get a friend to rehearse the interview the night before, by asking you questions that are likely to occur.

What questions do you need to answer?

Generally speaking your application form or curriculum vitae will set the agenda for the interview. The questions will be concerned with the following.

1. *The reason for your application.* The interviewer will try to assess your motivation and level of interest in the company and in the job itself.

2. *Your educational qualifications.* Be prepared to talk about your successes and failures, your best subjects along with the others. The interviewer may well be making judgements about your attitude to education as well as your achievements.

3. *Your previous work experience.* This is the key area for discussion in any job interview. Interviewers will want to quiz you about all aspects of your work experience: reasons for leaving previous jobs, the exact nature of your work, your level of responsibility, your attitudes to leadership and management. They will certainly ask probing questions about any gaps in your employment record and will want you to clarify your reasons for any job or career changes. In general, they will be trying to assess your level of commitment and honesty, and the kinds of working relationship with people that you normally establish.

4. *Your interests.* Expect some questions about how you spend your leisure time, your hobbies and interests. The interviewer will expect you to talk intelligently about your interests and will hope to derive some sense of your personality from these.

5. *Your capacity to perform the job in question.* This will be the question at the forefront of the interviewer's mind, so be prepared for questions that try to gauge your potential as an employee. Inviting you to place yourself in hypothetical situations, for example, 'How would you react if . . . ', is a common way of approaching this kind of question.

From *Punch*, 25 March 1985. Reprinted by permission.

In addition to the overt concerns that are reflected in the questions, there is also a hidden agenda which is seldom openly discussed, but is nonetheless in the interviewer's mind.

★ *Your motivation.* On balance, employers are looking for willing workhorses rather than galley slaves and they know that enthusiasm and motivation are important. Your commitment to the job is of prime concern to the interviewer.

★ *Your plans and intentions.* Recruiting staff is a costly business in terms of media advertising, agency fees and staff time. Recruiters are going to want to be sure that *(a)* you will take the job if it is offered and *(b)* that you will stay long enough for them to get some return for any training you receive. Any hint that you regard a permanent job as a short-stay adventure may cost you the job.

★ *Will they get you at the price?* In a section of the job market where there are too few applicants and lots of vacancies, for example, companies will want to be sure that they can recruit you in face of the competition. They may well ask about your other job applications to see how serious a proposition you represent.

★ *Your ability to fit in to their organization.* Organizations, particularly the larger ones, have their own distinctive style and culture. British Rail, British Telecom and British Petroleum may all have very different cultural norms and the interviewer's job, implicitly, is to recruit people who are likely to fit in with everyone else in the company. This is the interviewer's final task. And this could explain why research has shown that appearance is such a crucial determining factor. Many interviewers are said to have made their decision about the candidate's suitability only minutes after the interview has started.

During the interview itself: some dos and don'ts

Apart from obvious points like punctuality and dress, these are the ones which are worth bearing in mind.

1. *Speech and body posture.* Make sure you are relaxed, but do not overdo it. Make yourself as comfortable as you can and be sure not to nurse documents, bags, and cups of tea on your

lap all at the same time. Speak clearly, looking at the inter-viewer(s) directly and be aware of background noise so that you can raise the tone of your voice if necessary. Be aware of your own verbal mannerisms and avoid the use of slang or inappropriate jargon.

2. *Give full and interesting answers.* Never answer simply 'Yes' or 'No' but override this kind of questioning and show that you are in charge of the situation by elaborating a little. It is always difficult to gauge exactly how long you should talk in reply to each question, but aim to achieve a balance. If the interviewers are shuffling their papers it means that they are bored and you have probably gone on for too long.

3. *Be positive.* There is a skill in emphasizing your strengths without appearing to do so. Some writers have called it 'boasting modestly'. It is a way of identifying your achieve-ments and the positive aspects of your life to date, almost by inference. For example, 'Although I was quite young at the time, I was given a fair degree of responsibility'. Do not belittle your experience, 'It gave me an insight into production processes' sounds very different from 'It was boring, routine assembly work'.

4. *Show that you can listen.* Many interviewers will want to tell you something about their organization. Show that you are interested. If you find yourself with a poor interviewer who talks for most of the time, look interested and try to override their monologue, when appropriate.

5. *Be precise* . . . in answering questions about the timing of your work experience and details of your educational record. An interviewer may well ask factual questions even though your application form is on the desk in front of him or her.

6. *Be honest* . . . about the range of your knowledge. If you say you know about a product or manufacturing process, and you do not, you may well be exposed in a later technical interview.

7. *Do not jump in with an answer to a question.* Wait until the interviewer has finished asking it.

8. *If you are asked a difficult question* . . . Ask the interviewer to rephrase or clarify what they have said. It is perfectly legitimate to maintain silence for a while and say, 'There are some issues in your question I need to think about for a moment'.

9. *If you feel you have answered a question badly* . . . You can always correct yourself by saying, 'That didn't quite come out as I meant it. What I really meant to say was . . . '.

10. *If you are asked to express opinions* . . . Aim to produce a balanced answer which accepts a range of opinions. Try not to be dogmatic.

11. *If you do not like the interview style* . . . There is probably little to be gained by confronting the interviewer during the interview. You can, however, always complain to his or her manager after the event in writing or by phone.

12. *If you suspect that questions you have been asked are not within the spirit of the law* (for example, 'Are you married?') . . . Again, there is little to be gained by challenging the interviewer. Leave it until the interview is over.

13. *If you become certain during the interview that the job is not right for you* . . . It is perfectly legitimate to terminate the interview before the interviewer draws it to a close by saying, 'I realize that this job is not what I had in mind. I really don't want to waste any more of your time . . . '.

14. *Ask questions.* At the final phase of the interview it is the usual practice for the interviewer to invite questions from the candidate. Have some of these prepared beforehand. You can refer to comments the interviewer may have made earlier or anything else that concerns you. It is usual to ask about: **location, training, salary, career development, relocation, associates, performance.**

    If possible, ask questions in a way which reflects your motivation. As well as those concerning the job and your personal prospects, it is perfectly legitimate to ask about the company's activities – its policies, products and even its performance. Any negotiation about salary and conditions of employment will probably start once the job is offered, so that it is probably not worth attempting to do deals at the end of your first interview.

Selection tests

In addition to interviews, many companies use selection tests to discover if applicants have the skills, intelligence or aptitude appropriate to a particular kind of work. If you are applying for a job as a trainee computer programmer, for an engineering or technical training scheme, for entry to the armed services or a large organization such as the Civil Service, it is very likely that you will have to undergo a selection test of some kind.

Tests of aptitude are used to measure an individual's potential for a specific kind of work. The kind of test used will therefore depend on the nature of the job and what the employer is looking for. Computer aptitude tests for programming personnel, and mechanical aptitude tests for engineering technicians are widely used. For many management jobs, applicants may be asked to complete a personality test as well as a test of all-round mental ability.

What kinds of question are involved? To be of any predictive value test items have to be confidential to the test producer and authorized user. It would undermine their value if they were widely available so that the potential applicants could get plenty of practice at answering them. It is for this reason that the exact content of psychological tests is not widely publicized. It is possible, however, to point to the *kinds* of question that are commonly used in some selection tests.

Many tests of general ability will include three different types of question or subtest to measure your performance:

Tests of *verbal reasoning* are designed to measure your ability to analyse facts objectively. A short passage of writing, perhaps from a newspaper or journal, may be given, followed by a number of statements which you will be asked to evaluate and indicate whether they are true and logically correct, or untrue. Some tests of verbal reasoning may also test your knowledge of word meanings.

Tests of *numerical or quantitative reasoning* are designed to measure your ability to make calculations, decisions or inferences from numerical and statistical data. You may be asked to work out a solution to a given problem and then indicate which of a list of answers is correct.

Tests of *spatial ability* are used to measure abstract reasoning. The items, common to many IQ and intelligence tests, invite the person being tested to look at a series of shapes and patterns and then decide what kind of pattern should follow next in the sequence.

What is the best way to do the tests and are they important? Most test results are used as *part* of the selection process and so, if you score badly, it does not necessarily mean that you will fail to get the job. Much will depend on how you perform at interview.

How should you prepare for tests? Most have fixed time limits and speed and accuracy are important. It is therefore important to keep a clear head and be reasonably alert when you take them. If you get stuck on any one question for a long time, move on to the next question. Many applicants ask whether it is advisable to answer randomly or guess if they begin to run out of time. It is not likely that mere guessing will improve your score, particularly as wrong answers may well be deducted from your final score.

Assessment and selection centre methods

Many companies now use a form of selection which is considerably more elaborate than the one-to-one interview. It is called an *assessment centre*. Typically, these events last for a day or more and include interviews, tests, and group and individual exercises. They are used particularly in management selection and by large organizations such as the Civil Service.

The exercises may take several forms. 'In-tray' exercises invite candidates to deal with the contents of an in-tray, for example, to prepare some information, or answer a letter of complaint. Some job simulation exercises may be more job specific. Budget decision exercises, for example, may be used for selection to posts in management accounting. The aim of these exercises is simply to see how candidates might perform in real-life job situations.

In addition, group exercises are often used to see how candidates relate to other people around them. Group discussion and decision making exercises are frequently used to demonstrate social and communication skills. Officer selection methods in the armed services rely heavily on group exercises, often to do with logistics and problem solving. Typically, candidates have to manoeuvre six or seven other candidates around an obstacle course, using a plank of wood and a length of rope. But group exercises such as these are simply one part of a total programme of tests and interviews and a candidate's rating is likely to be based on performance over the whole programme.

From the candidate's point of view, selection/assessment centres can be stressful and anxiety inducing. It is often difficult to perform as you would like to in a competitive situation in which you are unsure of the ground rules. Are the recruiters looking for dominant leaders or effective group members? How can you judge what is successful performance? Some companies will give advance information to candidates to explain the purposes of the selection centre in order to try and diffuse anxiety. Some may even give examples of test items so that candidates can be prepared for test sessions.

On the whole, advice from the recruiters seems to be that in group exercises candidates should, where possible, 'be themselves' and participate as confidently as they can. There are no points awarded, it seems, for being dominant or aggressive. So what are the assessors looking for? The following list may give you some idea of the kinds of attribute or behaviour that observers could be looking for.

★ *Degree of participation*. How far did the applicant take part in the proceedings?

★ *Influence on others*. Was the applicant's point of view accepted?

★ *Oral expression*. Did the applicant speak clearly?

★ *Quality of thought*. Could the applicant analyse the problem and grasp the essential points?

★ *Determination*. How far did the applicant apply him or herself?

★ *Originality*. Was the applicant able to contribute any new ideas?

Whether or not you are successful, this kind of selection method can provide a powerful learning experience. It will therefore help to share your experience with someone after the event.

The interview outcome

So what of the interview outcome? How have you fared?

If you are not successful at a job interview you may need to balance your feelings of disappointment with the idea that the interview experience may have taught you something about yourself that you did not already know. In one obvious sense, the process of going to interviews enables you to research potential employers and test out your career ideas. Interviews can act as a catalyst for career decision making. Remember also that a single rejection does not imply that you are not right for the job. The successful candidate may have marginally more in the way of relevant experience. Selection decisions are often finely balanced and often there are a number of perfectly eligible candidates. However, if you find you have had several interviews without a single offer, you may need to improve your interview skills, or even question your suitability for the kind of work you have been seeking. Perhaps it is time to review your career goals.

If you have been successful in getting a job offer, you may well be weighing up the implications of accepting it and reading the fine print of the terms and conditions of employment. If there are elements in the job package that are not acceptable, now is the time to start negotiating a better deal. If, for example, you obtain two job offers and the one you prefer has the lower salary, you can explain the situation to the prospective employer and possibly negotiate a higher starting salary.

Conclusion

It is perhaps tempting to see the job offer as an end point in the career planning process and to view the prospect of a new job as a chance to relax and freewheel; time to file away your **Personal and Career Profile**, your notes on job search, and the replies from prospective employers.

But even if you have been successful at starting out on your chosen career, returning to work after a break, or negotiating a career change, it is important to keep your career planning skills in play to watch that you are heading in the direction that is right for *you*. You will need to keep reviewing your goals.

Having clearly defined goals is important for your confidence, motivation and sense of self worth. The more you are able to state what you want from a career, to plan a strategy and to identify supporting resources, the more likely it is that you will be successful in managing changes to your satisfaction. The skills of self appraisal, researching opportunities for personal and career development and of marketing yourself can be brought into play time and again. They need to be rehearsed continually. In particular your career plan will require continual revision and updating, to encompass unforeseen events and situations.

Career planning thus becomes an ongoing, lifelong process, of which *YOU* are in control.

INFORMATION SOURCES

Job ideas

Equal Opportunities: A Careers Guide (1987) by Ruth Miller and Anna Alston. A comprehensive careers encyclopedia. (Penguin Books, Harmondsworth.)

Occupations An annual directory of 600 jobs with simple job descriptions and training routes, giving the qualifications required for entry. (Careers and Occupational Information Centre, Sheffield.)

Working In . . . ' A series of booklets giving an insight into the day-to-day acticities of various occupations, ranging from work with animals to TV and video. (Careers and Occupational Information Centre, Sheffield.)

Education and training

The Directory of Further Education Annual listing of courses at colleges of technology and further education in the UK. (Careers Research and Advisory Centre, Hobsons Publishing, Cambridge.)

Higher Education – Finding your Way (1988) By David Dixon. A simple introductory guide to institutions, qualifications and grants. (Her Majesty's Stationery Office, London.)

The Polytechnic Courses Handbook Annual publication. (Committee of Directors of Polytechnics, London.)

Second Chances (1987) by Andrew Pates and Martin Good. Looks at the range of education and training options open to adults. (Careers and Occupational Information Centre, Sheffield.)

University Entrance Annual publication. (Association of Commonwealth Universities, London.)

Which Degree? (1988) Information on all university, polytechnic and college of higher education first degree courses. (Newpoint Publishing, London.)

Self employment

Coping with Starting a Business (1987) by Helen Steadman. A 'hints and tips' guide to starting out on your own. Mainly written with graduates in mind. (Newpoint Publishing, London.)

Starting a Business on a Shoestring (1988) by Michel Syrett and Chris Dunn. The most thorough and comprehensive guide to self employment presently available. (Penguin Books, Harmondsworth.)

Starting your own Business (1986) Strong on the practical aspects of self employment. (Consumers' Association, London.)

Researching particular companies

Graduate Employment and Training Annual. (CRAC, Hobsons Publishing, Cambridge.)

Graduate Opportunities Annual. (Newpoint Publishing, London.)

The Job Book Annual publication giving details of the main employers and training organisations. (CRAC, Hobsons Publishing, Cambridge.)

The Kompass Register Annual. A guide to manufacturers and producers in the UK which also lists companies according to geographical area. (Kompass Publishers, East Grinstead.)

Register of Graduate Employment and Training Annual directory of the main graduate recruiters. (Central Services Unit, Manchester.)

Returning to work

Part-Time Work (1986) by Judith Humphries. A clear guide to job finding and benefits. (Kogan Page, London).

Return to Work – Education and Training for Women (1987) A Directory of courses designed for women who want to return to work. Collated by the Women Returners Network. (Longman Group, Harlow.)

Unemployment

The New Unemployment Handbook (1987) by Guy Dauncey and Jane Mountain. A practical handbook with chapters on time use and survival strategies as well as job hunting. (National Extension College, Cambridge.)

The Penguin Guide to Supplementary Benefits (1985) by Tony Lynes. (Penguin, Harmondsworth.)

Job hunting
Job Hunting for Women (1986) by Margaret Wallis, Directed mainly towards women graduates. (Kogan Page, London.)

What Colour is your Parachute? (1983) by Richard Nelson Bolles. A comprehensive job search reader, but written mainly for the American market. (Ten Speed Press, Berkeley Ca., distributed by Airlift Books, London.)

PLACEMENT AND HELPING AGENCIES

If you want some professional advice to help you generate career ideas and suggestions, you could turn to some of the agencies listed below. But remember:

1. No *one* centre is likely to have all the information and expertise you require. They all cater for different clients and have a slightly different remit, and you may well have to use a number of different agencies to meet your needs.

2. The quality of the help you get varies tremendously from agency to agency. So be prepared for this and don't be too disappointed if you are unable to find quick and easy solutions to your career problem.

Most of the agencies listed may be able to provide information and suggestions for future action, but ultimately the final decision is **yours.** No one else can make it for you.

Education guidance services for adults A number of free agencies exist which help adults with information about continuing education. Over 70 local authorities now provide the general public with information and advice about the range of continuing education opportunities on offer. The service is free.

Professional and Executive Recruitment (PER) used to be part of the public employment service. Now privatized, it handles vacancies and provides a free service to job seekers including a jobs newspaper and supporting seminars. As the name implies, PER offices deal mainly in management and professional jobs.

Recruitment agencies and consultancies earn their money by charging employers to recruit or preselect applicants on a company's behalf. They may handle job vacancies that are not featured in press advertising. Some will specialize in a particular kind of vacancy, for example, accountancy or computing. Others will specialize in short-term or temporary jobs. Individuals can register with agencies free of charge.

The careers service Local education authority Careers Services provide a careers advisory and placement service to young people in school and college or for those who have recently completed their studies. Their services are free and range from individual advisory interviews and computer based guidance programmes to job placement and the provision of careers information. Careers officers should have a good knowledge of the local job market and the kinds of opportunity, including YTS, that exist. Careers services do not generally help adults either in or out of work.

Job Centres are also part of the public employment service. They mainly handle opportunities in clerical, craft and sales occupations and unskilled jobs of every kind. They also have information about the government's various special employment programmes.

Vocational guidance agencies A number of fee-charging agencies exist which invite you to undertake a range of psychological tests of personality, interest and aptitude. On the basis of the test results and a guidance interview, their staff will make recommendations about appropriate career options. Clients are then provided with a written summary. It is perhaps worth ensuring that the staff running the agency are professionally qualified, if you want to get value for your money.

Careers advisory services in colleges, polytechnics and universities All polytechnics and universities and most colleges have their own careers advisory and counselling services which provide careers information, individual counselling and help in job finding, arising from their extensive contact with employers of graduates. They also give advice on self marketing, compiling c.v.s and interview preparation. Their services are free to present and former students.

JOB FAMILIES

The list of jobs which follows has been designed to complement the **Job Interests Profile** in Part 2. Under each job interest heading a simple list of job titles illustrates the range of jobs available. As a rule, the jobs at the top of each list require only basic qualifications and training. Those lower down the list require progressively more in the way of qualifications and entry requirements. (The list is taken from Carpenter *et al. Your GCSE Decisions,* published by Careers Consultants Ltd., Richmond, Surrey. Reprinted by permission.)

As with any listing, there are some obvious omissions. Where, I hear you say, are careers in the uniformed services? Why is there not a section on outdoor work? The simple answer is that some jobs are more easily classifiable than others; and the listing is designed to be illustrative rather than exhaustive.

To get further information about any of the jobs mentioned, you can turn to the reference books listed in *Information Sources.*

PEOPLE/SOCIAL

In health and personal services . . .

Ambulance Staff, Hospital Porter
Nursing Auxiliary
Hairdresser
Dental Surgery Assistant
Beautician/Beauty Therapist
Enrolled Nurse

In sales . . .

Shop Assistant/Sales Assistant/
Cashier
Hotel Receptionist
Telephone Sales Clerk
Sales Representative

In the community . . .

Residential Care Worker
(e.g. homes for elderly)
Health Visitor
Community Worker
Charities Organizer
Religious Minister
Social Worker/Medical Social
Worker
Probation Officer
Psychologist

With children or young people . . .

Nursery Nurse
Sick Children's Nurse (RSCN)
Education Welfare Officer
Youth Worker
Teacher
Careers Officer
Educational Psychologist

RESEARCH/SCIENTIFIC

In science . . .

Laboratory Assistant
Laboratory Technician
Metallurgical Technician
Industrial Chemist/Food Scientist/
Pharmaceutical Scientist
Biologist/Biochemist/Physicist
Astronomer/Astrophysicist/
Mathematician/Statistician
Geologist/Geophysicist/
Meteorologist/Matallurgist
Materials Scientist/Environmental
Scientist/Ecologist/Information
Scientist
Technical Writer

In computing . . .

Data Processing Operator/Clerk
Computer Operator
Computer Programmer
Systems Analyst
Computer Engineer

In health . . .

Dental Technician
Dental Hygienist
Physiological Measurement
Technician (cardiology, audiology,
etc.)
Registered Nurse (RGN, RMN,
RNMH)
Dispensing Optician
Pharmacy Technician/Dispenser
Medical Laboratory Scientific Officer
Chiropodist
Radiographer
Occupational Therapist
Physiotherapist
Speech Therapist
Orthoptist
Dietician
Ophthalmic Optician
Pharmacist
Dentist
Osteopath/Chiropractor
Doctor

ARTISTIC/CREATIVE

In design . . .

Window Dresser
Florist
Photographer
Press Photographer
Artist
Designer (graphic, fashion, interior,
etc.)
Technical Illustrator
Art Teacher
Art Historian/Art Gallery Manager

In performance . . .

Actor
Dancer
Fashion/Photographic Model
Singer/Musician
Professional Sportsperson
Lighting Technician (theatre)
Stage Manager
Sound Technician (radio/TV)
TV Camera Operator
Studio Manager
Make-up Artist
Film Editor (TV)
Sports Centre Manager
Stage Designer
Broadcasting Engineer

With the written word . . .

Author
Library Assistant/Information
Assistant
Journalist
Museum Assistant
Museum Conservation Technician
Publisher/Editor
Information Officer/Public Relations
Officer
Librarian
Interpreter/Translator
Museum Curator
Archaeologist
Archivist

ENGINEERING/PRACTICAL

In construction . . .

Builder's Labourer
Bricklayer/Carpenter/Plumber/
Plasterer
Painter and Decorator
Electrician
Architectural/Surveying Technician
Estimator
Building Technician
Cartographic Draughtsperson
Building Surveyor
Building Technologist/Site Manager
Cartographer
Surveyor
Town Planner
Architect

In manufacturing . . .

Production Worker (unskilled/
semiskilled)
Production Worker (skilled)
Packer
Machinist
Baker
Foundry Worker
Woodworking Machinist/Furniture
Maker
Printing Worker
Industrial Technician
Production Manager
Industrial Technologist
Engineering Operator
Sheet Metral Worker/Welder
Vehicle Mechanic
Engineering Craftsperson (fitter,
toolmaker, etc.)
Engineering Technician/
Draughtsperson
Technician Engineer
Professional/Chartered Engineer

In leisure . . .

Domestic Staff
Kitchen Staff
Waiting Staff
Chef/Cook

BUSINESS/ORGANIZING

In finance . . .

Bank Clerk, Building Society Clerk,
Insurance Clerk
Accountancy Technician
Insurance Agent/Inspector
Insurance Broker/Underwriter
Banker/Bank Manager/Building
Society Manager
Accountant (chartered, certified,
management, public finance)
Actuary
Stockbroker
Investment Analyst

In sales . . .

Store Supervisor
Market Research Interviewer
Retail Manager
Retail Buyer
Advertising Copy-writer
Marketing Manager
Market Research Analyst/Executive

In administration . . .

Telephonist
Typist/Word Processor Operator
Clerical Assistant (Civil Service, local
government, Health Service)
Secretary
Specialist Secretary (medical, legal,
agricultural)
Clerical Officer
Bilingual Secretary
Executive Officer (Civil Service or
Post Office)
Local Government Administrative
Trainee/Officer
Administrative/Business
Management Trainee (Health
Service, industry and commerce)
Personnel Officer
Chartered/Company Secretary
Tax Inspector

In leisure . . .

Hotel/Housekeeper
Fast Food Shop Manager
Hotel/Catering Manager
Home Economist

INDEX